Fourth Edition

Business Communication
on the Edge of Technology

|| Jackie Martin ||

Kendall Hunt
publishing company

Cover image © Shutterstock, Inc.

Kendall Hunt
publishing company

www.kendallhunt.com
Send all inquiries to:
4050 Westmark Drive
Dubuque, IA 52004-1840

Dedication

Students:

This book is dedicated to you, to your academic and professional growth, and to your future endeavors.

The classroom is a dynamic and organic example of the communication process. No two classes are ever the same! It is my pleasure to both disseminate and graciously receive information and feedback from the perpetually interesting and talented students who pass through my classroom doors—and my life—each semester. You have all left a little piece of yourselves with me, and I have learned much from you. Teaching truly is a mutual exchange. We all gain in life experience as well as academics in the classroom.

I sincerely hope that this text helps you gain practical knowledge while transitioning into the business world. As always, stay on the cutting edge!

Professor Martin

Contents

Author's Opening Message to Students. xi

Note to Instructors xiii

CHAPTER *One* **Communications in Business**   **1**

The Importance of Communication, and the End Goal 3

The Communication Cycle 5

Practicing the Six Steps of the Transformational Leadership
    Communication Cycle 8

Organizational Communication Styles and Structures. 10

CHAPTER *Two* **Using Technology to Deliver the Message Successfully**   **23**

Intent Dictates Form and Expectation Affects Reception 25

Technology and Communication 25

Current Business Communication Forms. 27

Business Communication Documents and Technologies. 29

Planning 37

The Planning Process According to Document Form. 38

Standard Hard Copy Business Documents 39

Basic Business Letters. 40
    Block Style   40
    Modified Block Style Business Letter   44

Basic Business Memorandums 44
    Memorandum Block   44
    Composing an Electronic or E-mail Document   49
    E-mail Attachments   49

Text Messages 49

Bulk SMS or Bulk Text Messages 51

Instant Messaging (IM). 52

Tweets 52

Blogs 53

CHAPTER *Three*   **Composition: Sentence, Paragraph and Whole Document Considerations**   **61**

Composition 63

Audience and Adaptation 64

Building Concise and Clear Sentences 65
        Word Choice   65
        Slang   65
        Discriminatory Language   65
        Gender and Age Neutral Language   67
        Clichés and Idioms   69
        Active vs. Passive Voice   69

Sentence Design 73
        Organize the Sentence   75
        Use Supporting Examples   77
        Create Emphasis   77
        Avoid Dangling Modifiers   78
        Avoid Misplaced Modifiers   78
        Avoid Confusing Words Pairs   79
        Using Clarity to Build Concise and Clear Sentences   79
        Sentence Length   80
        Sentence Fluency   82

Creating the Excellent Paragraph 82
        Building Paragraphs That Flow with Transitions   83
        Building Parallelism and Balance   83
        Paragraph Length   86

Whole Document Considerations. 86

Final Formatting Considerations 86

The Response 86

Feedback: A New Step in the 3-Step Writing Process.
    Revision, Changing Behavior and Follow-up. 87

CHAPTER *Four*

Positive News, Neutral News, Bad News Messages, Persuasive Messages, and Reports   89

The Routine Inquiry 91

The Response to a Routine Inquiry 92
    Positive Response to a Routine Inquiry   92
    The Refused Request—A Negative Response to a Routine Inquiry   94

Adjustment Grants—Delivering Good News in Response to a Claim 95

Adjustment Grants—Delivering Bad News in Response to a Claim
    That Is Denied 96

Messages That Build Good Will 97
    Online Orders and Acknowledgements   97
    Good Will Messages of Praise or Congratulations   98

Persuasive Messages 99
    The AIDA approach   100

Persuasive Requests 101
    Setting Up the Explanation   101
    Using a Problem, Solution Approach   104

Sales Messages 105
    Creating and Delivering the Effective Sales Message   105
    Creating the Effective Sales Campaign   108
    Best Practices Planning Questions   108
    Presenting the Sales Message   109
    Social Media and Online Advertising and E-mail
      Marketing Campaigns   110
    Analyzing the Results   110

RFP Proposals 111

CHAPTER *Five* **The Report Cycle and the Use of Technology
to Enhance Reports**   **139**

The Report Cycle 141

Report Format 143

Use of Technology to Enhance Reports 143

To Apply Color and Graphic Design 147

Short Reports 159

Formal Reports 160

   Referencing Methods   164
   The Problem-Solving Process   165
   Research Methods   166
   Surveys   167
   Direct Observation   169
   Experimentation   169
   Secondary Data   170
   Collaborative Reports   171
   Strategies for Group Writing   172

CHAPTER *Six* **Communicating Orally**   **181**

When Interpersonal Communication Fails 183

   Sending Your Message Across the Divide—Communicating
      with an Edge   184
   The Importance of Phone Skills   185
   Communicating Effectively in Meetings   187
   Leading Effectively in Meetings   188
   Oral Communication with Formal Presentations   190
   PowerPoint Presentation Tips and Techniques   195
   Communication in the Workplace Categorized   198

CHAPTER *Seven* **Job Search, The E-Portfolio: "Branding" Yourself**   **203**

The Resume, First Impressions DO Count! 205

   Current Industry Standard Resumes   205
   Current Resume Writing Practice—Where To Find It   206

Personal Information   206

The Importance of the Summary Statement or Summary
    of Qualifications   207

Skills   210

Education and Certifications   212

References   217

Formatting the Resume 218
    What the Employer May Want to See   220

The Electronic Career Portfolio (EPortfolio) 220

Removing the First Potential Roadblock: Writing a Winning
    Cover Letter. 223
    Traditional Cover Letter   224
    E-mail Cover Letter   225

CHAPTER *Eight* **Are You Prepared for Today's Job Search?**
Job Search Strategies and the Interview Process   **229**

Digital Information Literacy. 231
    Assessments and Certifications as an Integral Part
        of the Interview Process   232

Job Search Strategies 234
    Active and Passive Job Search   234
    Networking   235

The Interview 235
    Interview Formats   243
    Salary and Benefits   243
    Follow-up   244
    Continued Career Development   244

Works Cited   **245**

Credits   **249**

Index   **251**

Author's Opening Message to Students

Business Communication on the Edge of Technology will teach you how to write with an edge, producing writing that is concise, succinct, and, most importantly, that gets the intended message across to the reader. It will also put you on the cutting edge of technology by teaching you to employ computer and Web-based writing tools effectively. Additionally, the text will direct you in fine-tuning the tone, quality, and intent of your message so that you will become a better communicator, and be perceived as such in your workplace. Given the technological information age in which we conduct business today, you need to be on that cutting edge.

We will discuss Business Communication in more traditional forms, but also incorporate Internet Business Communication or iBusiness Communication. Much of our communications today occur via the Internet and are even being conducted "on" the Internet through cloud computing, with users accessing applications and data through their browsers. In spite of the ever-changing technological tools that we employ to deliver our message, the need to produce good writing, regardless of the medium, is still fundamental to effective business communication. The written and spoken word, whether delivered through pencil and paper or via technology, has to be well written and concise, so that the message is received as it was intended.

Laura Micciche (2004) makes a strong and valid case for teaching rhetorical grammar.

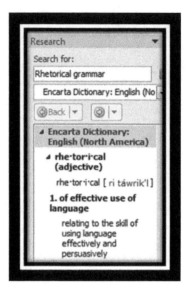

"*The absence of a sustained contemporary conversation about grammar instruction at the college level does not eclipse the practical reality that nearly every writing teacher struggles with at one time or another: how to teach students to communicate effectively. And effective communication, which entails grammar knowledge, is essential to achieving many of the goals regularly articulated in composition studies. Chief among them are teaching students to produce effective writing that has some relevancy to the world we live in, to see language as having an empowering and some-times transformative potential, and to critique normalizing discourses that conceal oppressive functions.*" (Micciche, p. 718)

"Rhetorical grammar instruction," she goes on to argue, "is just as central to composition's driving commitment to teach critical thinking and cultural critique as is reading rhetorically, understanding the significance of cultural difference, and engaging in community work through service-learning initiatives."

Note to Instructors

This course can be taught in a traditional face-to-face fashion, or as on online course. I personally achieve excellent results teaching this class in a computer classroom, having students using tools such as Word, Excel, Adobe Acrobat, Word Press, the Internet, and a dedicated classroom blog to practice their writing skills.

In an online format, markup tools in Word, sound files used to record and upload feedback to students, and narrations in PowerPoint for oral presentations, are tools and methodologies that meet new statewide Transfer Model Curriculum Standards.

Chapter One

Communications in Business

teamwork support

strategy

decision

ethic vision integrity

Leadership

contribution communication

motivation

influence

responsibility

planning management

Learning Objectives

LO1 Understand the importance of communication in the workplace.

LO2 Examine various communication cycles.

LO3 Practice engaging in transformational communication.

LO4 Describe organizational communication styles and structures.

The Importance of Communication, and the End Goal

We all know that effective communication is important to us. We feel better when communication is positive, when there is warmth and laughter, compassion and understanding, from those we hold in high regard. Given that our workplace is a second home, does it not seem desirable that we would wish for that same comfort level to be present at work? In this text, we will explore why communication is important in the work place, and why communication is important to you, as a vital component of that organizational team. Although most people would agree that communication is important, people are often not as effective as they could be in their communications. Perhaps messages are not received as intended and perhaps those messages may have unwanted results. Effective communication leads to effective organizational fluency, customer satisfaction, and profit. This is a model for success.

For you, as a team member in that organization, it is important to get along with your peers, supervisors, and subordinates. Greg Taffet and other Information Technology (IT) leaders want more than just IT skills in their new college graduates. In an article on the six key skills new IT grads are lacking, they continue to value what most businesses have cited for years—the "soft skills," particularly communication skills, leadership and teamwork (Pratt).

Profit is the "bottom line" in business language. Employees value an incentive such as a salary increase for a job well done. However, it may be surprising to know that though a salary increase is a highly motivating factor, acknowledgement and praise of a job well performed increases job performance even more. Effective communication most certainly is a highly valued business skill.

 Professor and Students: "Thought Bubble" means take a break and discuss these questions. Alternatively, blog about it at a blog site as instructed by your professor.

What is the "mission statement" of a company or organization? Find examples of mission statements online for a particular college or company of your choice.

What steps can we take in our professional lives to bring about positive, fluent communications, and how might we mirror those in our personal lives?

Let us take it a step further. We have established that positive communication is pleasant and desirable, and that it leads to productivity and profit. Positive communication is effective communication, and effective communication leads to efficiency and productivity in the organization. Moreover, effective communication leads to "engaged" employees. In an article in *Rural Telecommunications,* Droppers states that "Employees who understand the company's direction and know how to do their jobs to support that direction are more engaged; they have higher job satisfaction and overall morale, and are more productive." (Droppers, "Engage employees with effective communications")

This type of engagement does not happen by itself. It is a result of creating and employing effective role descriptions in the organization, which gives employees clarity as to their roles and creates a sense of ownership. When a specific person takes ownership over a task, there is a clear expectation as to who is going to complete the task. In a company or an organization, the Who, What, Where, When, and How of role descriptions is extremely important to successful communications. Role or job descriptions, scheduling, completion of tasks, tracking, project management, and follow-up are common tools that ensure a smooth and successful communication cycle. Let us look at the communication cycle and its elements and discuss how to ensure that the communication techniques you employ at work promote understanding of your "intended" message.

 If I understand my message, shouldn't everyone else? What incorrect assumptions might occur in this thinking process? (Discussion only)

As we will discuss next, there is more to ensuring that our communications are well received than thinking that they will be—simply because we understand the message. Communication takes many forms on its journey from Department A to Department Z, and in the end it may be interpreted as a "Plan A," and not your intended "Plan B." The intent of this text, and the activities that you will engage in throughout the course, will help you practice the skills that you need to ensure proper communication. First, let's take a brief look at the history behind the concept of the 'communication cycle' before moving into the skill set you will develop to improve your written and oral communication skills.

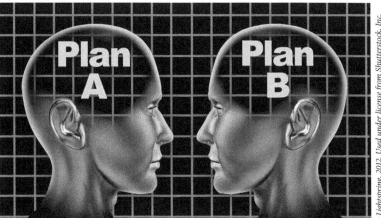

© Lightspring, 2012. Used under license from Shutterstock, Inc.

The Communication Cycle

The 'communication cycle' is the complete path of communication that occurs between sender and receiver. There have been several major models of the communication cycle since Claude Shannon and Warren Weaver developed a model for radio and telephone technologies, in which there were three primary parts: sender, channel, and receiver (Shannon). David Berlo expanded on Shannon and Weaver's linear model of communication with his Sender-Message-Channel-Receiver Model (Berlo). Wilbur Schramm noted that the impact that a message has on the target should also be examined (Schramm 3–26). More recently, a model called the transactional model of communication was proposed (Barnlund, A Transactional Model of Communication 47–57), which assumes the basic premise that individuals simultaneously engage in the sending and receiving of messages as displayed in Figure 1.

Finally, James MacGregor Burnes coined a communication model called 'transformational leadership' in his 1978 book titled "*Leadership.*" The model described research on political leadership, but it is now widely used in many leadership activities and takes various forms. It is generally used to improve productivity, performance, or profit (Burnes).

In Burnes' example, a six-step model is used to describe how leadership works (see Fig. 2, 'The Communication Cycle').

We will be examining these steps as they relate to communications in the workplace and to the writing process itself in further detail in Chapter 2. For now, let us begin with a discussion of the six steps.

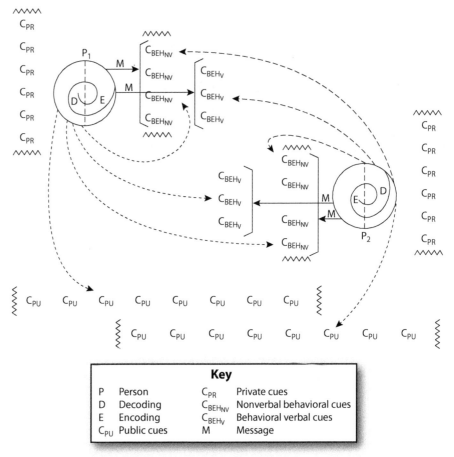

FIGURE 1 *(Barnlund, A Transactional Model of Communication)*

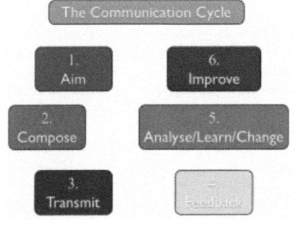

FIGURE 2 *The Communication Cycle.*

STEP 1. Aim—Who will you be addressing? In this step, you are considering your audience, their cultural level, corporate or organizational culture, and your motivations. What is the communication that you are trying to achieve? You will need to adapt your intended message to the audience. One way that you can "test" the reading level of your audience is to use the Word tool called "Readability Statistics."

STEP 2. Compose—What communication form will you use to communicate with your audience? The message itself may take many forms, such as: face-to-face, video, telephone, speech, voice mail, online, e-mail, letters, flyers, online media, electronic presentations, blogs, and social networking. Further, the importance of well-written documents is often overlooked and is a vital component of successful business communications.

STEP 3. Transmit—Where and when should you communicate in order to optimize your results? Timing is crucial in delivering a communication and having it be well received. For example, if you truly want your colleagues to study your document before the marketing meeting, then you will need to send it to them days in advance, not an hour before the meeting. Have you ever tried to deliver a key piece of information to your staff at 4:00 on a Friday afternoon, when people are "halfway out the door"? That message is better received on a Monday or a Tuesday morning when workers are fresh and ready to plan the week's activities. Yes, it is cliché, but we have all heard the expression "timing is everything." It certainly can be!

STEP 4. Feedback—What impact did your communication have? What feedback are you receiving because of your sent communication? If the feedback is negative or deviates from your point of view, sometimes it is hard to accept that point of view. However, you will learn and grow in any organization by asking for constructive feedback. Feedback is hard to accept, as it is this stage that prevents many communications from proceeding further in a positive fashion. It is only when we can move away from defensive reactions to feedback, and open ourselves to listening deeply, that we can actually internalize and synthesize so that we can adapt our writing for future communication. According to Fisher (2006), empathy, acceptance, congruence, and concreteness are the four qualities of active listening. In addition, the listener should deviate from this position and offer an opinion only if the other person asks for it.

STEP 5. Analyze/Learn/Change—Based on the feedback and result of your communication, analyze, synthesize, and discuss the information with colleagues and perhaps even with family and friends. Then make any necessary changes. Remember, in Step 4, we have already accepted the recommendations. In this step, you may actually have to conduct a bit of inquiry as well, based on the constructive feedback. There is a plethora of information on the Internet, so this necessary research has become easier. Based on your research, make the necessary changes to your documents. It is crucial to effective communication that you edit correspondence before sending, often many times, and ask others to review and make recommendations as well. Insufficient editing of written communications is a step that is not appreciated enough in business. We will practice *the crucial repetitive editing step* often throughout this text *to refine our writing.*

STEP 6. **Improve**—The emphasis in this step is on a positive change in your own behavior, and on taking ownership of that improvement. This should take the form of changes in your thinking, feelings, and actions.

 Do further research on one of the communication cycles listed above.

 Have you experienced a communication breakdown at your place of employment or in some other organization? Do you think your response improved future communications? If so, describe how your response improved communication. If not, describe how you might improve the communication cycle in the future. Explain.

Practicing the Six Steps of the Transformational Leadership Communication Cycle

Once you have an understanding of the communication cycle, consider how you can practice enhanced oral and written communication so that your message is well received and a positive end result is achieved:

STEP 1 *Consider your audience and adapt.*

What is the educational level, the age, and the cultural and perhaps religious background of your audience? Adapt your writing and speaking levels accordingly.

STEP 2 *Choose the form of communication and compose.*

Will you be speaking, giving a PowerPoint presentation, presenting a graph that shows significant company data, writing a memo, sending an e-mail to one or many, creating and supporting a Website, or collecting online data for analysis and distribution? The intent of the communication, the feedback you anticipate, and the tools and forms of communication available to the recipient are all important considerations.

STEP 3 *Choose when to transmit the message.*

You should transmit the message when people are most open to receiving it. A Friday afternoon may seem like the worst time to deliver it; however, many people now work from home and are online constantly, so you will need to pay attention to the "reading" habits of your audience. What time of the day does the individual seem to read and reply to your message? You'll also need to carefully consider just who should receive a copy of that message. It is just as injurious not to include someone in a message that is relevant or critical to her as it is to send the message to the wrong recipient. Be very careful to edit your communication many times and not to hit the "send" button too quickly. You cannot take that message back once it is sent!

STEP 4 *Receive and internalize feedback.*

How do we internalize feedback in order to effect changes in our behavior? We engage in reflective listening. According to Fisher (2006), we should listen more than talk, respond to what is personal rather than abstract, restate what the other has said, not ask questions or tell the listener what he or she feels or believes, try to understand the feelings and not just the facts, and empathize with the other's frame of reference.

By studying these important methods, and by practicing them, you will become a more reflective listener and be able to connect with your peers and coworkers.

STEP 5 *Refine your communications based on feedback.*

This text will allow you to spend an entire semester refining your written and verbal communications. By using the included activities, you will develop skills that will enhance your written and spoken communications even after you leave the classroom.

STEP 6 *Improve, change!*

Research leadership training in organizations helps you accelerate your ability to change. Many leadership training institutes, books, and seminars teach you how to lead and communicate effectively.

Changes should be reflected in the tone, emotion, and quality of your written and oral communications. This step is the hardest to achieve, but it has the biggest payoff. Remember that the end goal is to have the listener hear your communication as it was intended, and to achieve the result you desire. If it takes a few revisions to accomplish that, the time will be well spent.

For the next two activities, Assignment 4 and Assignment 5, please use the Tear Out Sheets at the end of this chapter.

 Practice Transformational Leadership Principles right now, in your class. Later, apply these techniques to your workplace, home, or interest group, or even blog about it at your classroom blog site.

 Reflective Listening Activity. Break into groups of five to ten students. Have two students volunteer to model the Reflective Listening process. Place two chairs in front of the group. Have the entire group decide on a situation that they have encountered at work or school or some other group to which they belong. Give them ten minutes to recall a scenario. Ask them to briefly describe it on paper. You may have students use the computer to compose this in Word. Do not put your name on the paper. Keep it anonymous. Tear your paper out of the text, after placing a number on the backside of the page, assigned by your instructor. Pass the paper to your left. Make comments on your peer's paper.

Organizational Communication Styles and Structures

We have already established that any organization, whether public or private, is both an economic system and a social system. A positive social system is crucial to the proper functioning of the economic system. Whether the organization is marketing a product for profit, or is a non-profit organization established to ensure a particular educational or charitable agenda, effective communication creates a positive social system and is vital to the success of the organization.

Several key factors determine how individuals interact within the social system. They are the culture of the organization, the emotional current of the organization, and the structure of the organization.

Organizational culture has received increasing attention from both scholars and business leaders. In particular, the field of empirical studies examining the connection between organizational culture and effectiveness is growing.[1] The culture of the organization determines the type of communication that should be used to achieve the desired result. Some companies and organizations, such as certain government branches, are very formal in their hierarchical structure; therefore, communications between workers are more formal in nature. In a less formal organization, especially those with a creative bent such as an advertising company, communications tend to be more relaxed and even unconventional by design. It is important to pay attention to culture and to adapt written and oral communications to fit the culture. We will learn to adapt written forms of communication to culture in Chapter 2.

Another factor that affects the tone of communications is the "emotional current" of an organization. The emotional current of the organization, or the prevailing feelings regarding current organizational issues, reflects how employees feel, and this feeling is conveyed in various forms of communication. If there is a negative internal message circulating, such as the announcement of a large layoff, this influences workers' morale. Internal communications, especially with the use of e-mail, may rapidly convey this negativity throughout the organization and in some cases may reach external stakeholders, such as shareholders and clients. It is important for leaders to be aware of this type of communication. Capitalizing on and promoting good news, such as the success of an idea or product, is as important as mitigating bad news.

One way in which the emotional climate of the organization manifests itself is referred to as the "grapevine." The grapevine is the informal network of communications that takes place between employees at the water cooler, around the copy machine, in the workroom, or in the hallways before or after a meeting. It is very important to be aware of this social network as it should in part dictate the next steps in the communication cycle. The form of communication to use, or even to abstain from using, is critical in this stage of the communication process.

---

[1] Denison and Mishra cite several empirical studies they have conducted on page 206 of their article, "Organizational Culture and Effectiveness."

Our final consideration is how organizational structure impacts communication choice. To illustrate this, we will refer to a common business graphic called the organizational chart.

Organizational charts represent the organizational structure that establishes the chain of command among various levels of employees. Similar charts can also be used to show the information flow of a new marketing product from concept to market, or to conduct project management, whereby resources are organized, allocated, and secured for a particular project that has a beginning and an end point in mind.

Consider the differences between these two organizational chart structures:

The first chart on the left shows a very traditional top-down management style. Conversely, the chart on the right shows a circular form of communication, where the management and production teams are enveloping the core of workers.

 How do you think the communication would vary between the two types of charts in Figure 3? Write a two paragraph response to this question using Microsoft Word. Save in a PDF format with your name, date, and assignment number, and upload to your online class site and/or print and give to your instructor.

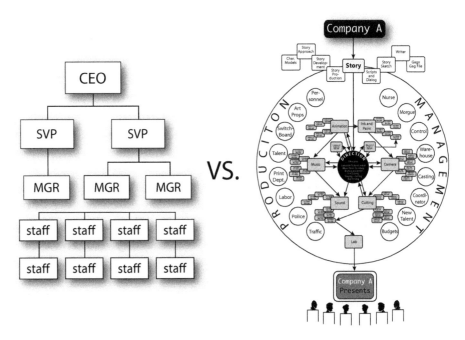

FIGURE 3 *Standard Organizational Chart vs. Circular Organizational Chart.*

Imagine that you are at a wedding with one hundred guests, and that there is just one long table with all guests seated on either side of that table. What do you think communication would be like in this case? Now imagine the same one hundred guests divided into ten tables of ten people and consider the communication that might take place with this table arrangement. Write a four paragraph response to this scenario using Microsoft Word. Spellcheck, save in PDF format with your name, date, and assignment number, and upload to your online class site.

 Using your favorite search engines, find an organizational chart structure that reflects an organization or a business to which you belong. Save with your name, date, and assignment number, and upload to your online class site.

The structure of an organization affects the way that people communicate in the organization. Often the product or the mission of the organization dictates the form of communication as well. Just as organizing tables and chairs into circles, as opposed to a straight line, will affect the type of communication that occurs at a meeting or event, the physical layout and hierarchical organization of a company impacts communication to enhance or impede the end goal.

Consider a more traditional hierarchical flow chart, such as a flow chart for the Department of Defense, where the chain of command needs to be clearly understood and followed, since discussing options in moments of international crisis may result in loss of life.

Quite distinct however, is an advertising organization, where the reporting chain would have design team members participating at the same "flat" level to encourage creative feedback and dialogue, with the Design Team Lead encouraging feedback from all members.

 Using the Insert SmartArt command, choose a hierarchy or a relationship to show the reporting structure of an organization or a company to which you belong.

Finally, communication, organizational culture, and emotional current are as dynamic as the individuals who make up the organization. Therefore, communication and culture changes, so we have to be aware of the changes, be willing to embrace them, and adapt.

U.S. DEPARTMENT OF DEFENSE

| HOME | TODAY IN DOD | ABOUT DOD | TOP ISSUES | NEWS | PHOTOS/VIDEOS |

- Secretary of Defense / Deputy Secretary of Defense
  - Chairman of the Joint Chiefs of Staff/Vice Chairman of the Joint Chiefs of Staff
    - Joint Chiefs of Staff
      - Chief of Naval Operations
      - Chief of Staff of the Air Force
      - Chief of Staff of the Army
      - Commandant of the Marine Corps
    - The Joint Staff - Director Joint Staff
      - Directorate of Management
      - J-1 Manpower and Personnel
      - J-2 Joint Staff Intelligence
      - J-3 Operations
      - J-4 Logistics
      - J-5 Strategic Plans and Policy
      - J-6 Command, Control, Communications, and Computer Systems
      - J-7 Operational Plans and Joint Force Development
      - J-8 Force Structure Resources and Assessment
  - Military Departments
    - Department of the Air Force - Secretary of the Air Force
      - Air Force Operating Commands and Agencies
    - Department of the Army - Secretary of the Army
      - Army Operating Commands and Agencies
    - Department of the Navy - Secretary of the Navy
      - Navy Operating Commands and Agencies
    - United States Marine Corps
      - Marine Corps Operating Commands and Agencies
  - Office of the Secretary of Defense
    - Department of Defense Executive Secretariat
    - Office of the Assistant Secretary of Defense for Legislative Affairs
    - Office of the Assistant Secretary of Defense for Networks and Information Integration/Chief Information Officer
    - Office of the Assistant Secretary of Defense for Public Affairs
    - Office of the Deputy Chief Management Officer
    - Office of the Director Cost Assessment and Program Evaluation
    - Office of the Director of Administration and Management
      - Defense Freedom of Information Policy Office
      - Historical Office of the Office of the Secretary of Defense
      - Pentagon Force Protection Agency
      - Washington Headquarters Service

FIGURE 4 *Traditional Top-Down Organizational Chart.*

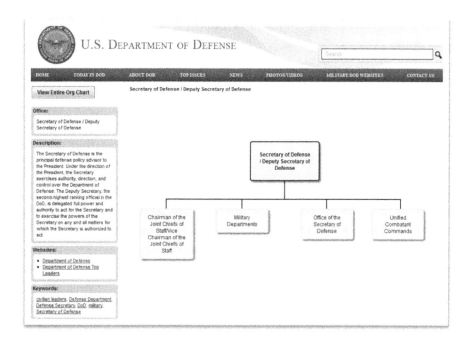

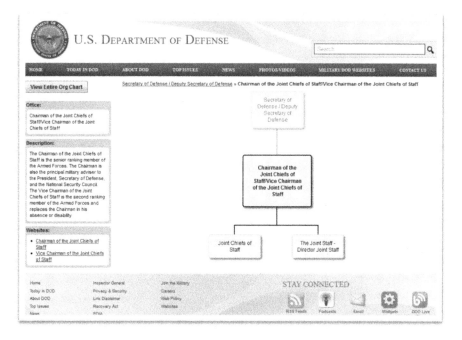

FIGURE 4 *continued*

Tall Organizational Structure

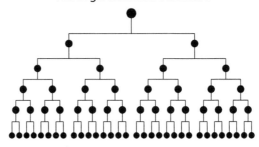

Flat Organizational Structure

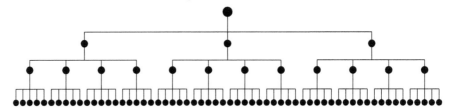

FIGURE 5 *Flat vs. Tall Organizational Hierarcy*

FIGURE 6 *Communication Changes*

Student Activity Pages

Scenario (Use the same case study throughout the book so that the same documents can be edited repetitively and adapted to different scenarios in chapters.)

> Mr. Smith, Sales Director
> Ms. Malloy, Marketing Director
> Mr. Ruiz, Marketing & Sales Manager
> Company: Business Writing With An Edge Consulting Group

■ Situation

Mr. Smith and Ms. Malloy have been coworkers for several years, working closely together. Over the past year, Mr. Smith and Ms. Malloy have engaged in a more personal relationship. Apparently, the relationship is not working out, so Ms. Malloy would like Mr. Smith to stop communicating with her through company e-mail. Mr. Smith does not want to end the relationship so he continues to send her personal e-mails, even after Ms. Malloy has asked him several times to stop.

As Mr. Smith continues, Ms. Malloy finally tires of this behavior, and she writes an e-mail memo to her supervisor, Mr. Ruiz, who also is Mr. Smith's supervisor. She threatens to sue the company if Mr. Smith does not stop corresponding with her using company e-mail. She states that she can no longer work closely with Mr. Smith and feels that his behavior will negatively affect the marketing campaign that they have been working on for over a year.

Mr. Ruiz decides to call a meeting with Mr. Smith alone first.

Discussion Considerations Should company e-mail be used for personal correspondence? To whom should Ms. Malloy have sent the e-mail? To whom should she not have sent the correspondence? What was her aim, her audience, her goal? What form of communication should she have used?

■ Notes to instructor

Feedback from Ms. Malloy's supervisor was negative, so should she use that to gauge future communication and to change her behavior? Ms. Malloy should realize she implicated herself by using company e-mail. She can improve by not using company e-mail, by having private conversations, and by involving HR if

Mr. Smith is harassing. Also, perhaps Ms. Malloy should have had a spoken conversation first with her supervisor, without using a threat of escalation.

Student Activity Tear Outs

"Six-Step Transformational Communication Cycle Activity Table"
Answer the following using the Six-Step Transformational Communication Cycle table in the Student Activity Tear Out Section:

 How should Ms. Malloy aim, compose, and transmit her message?

 After transmission of the message, how should she engage in the last three steps of the six-step transformational communication cycle?

SIX-STEP TRANSFORMATIONAL COMMUNICATION CYCLE ACTIVITY TABLE		
Aim	Compose	Transmit

SIX-STEP TRANSFORMATIONAL COMMUNICATION CYCLE ACTIVITY TABLE		
Receive Feedback	Analyze Learn Change	Improve

Do not put your name on the paper; keep it anonymous. Tear your paper out of the text, after placing a number on the backside of the page, assigned by your instructor. Pass the paper to your left. Make comments on your peer's paper.

Reflective Practice Reflective Listening. Engage in each step of the process, but pause to take
Listening notes on how you and your partner are interacting as you conduct the communi-
Activity cation exchange. Your topic during this process is the responses from the Student
Activity "six-step transformational communication cycle activity table."

Listen more than talk.

_____

_____

_____

_____

Respond to what is personal, rather than abstract.

_____

_____

_____

_____

Restate what your partner has said, do not ask questions or tell the listener what
he/she feels or believes.

_____

_____

_____

_____

Try to understand your partner's feelings, not just the facts.

_____

_____

_____

_____

Empathize with the other's frame of reference with acceptance.

_____

_____

_____

_____

The completed activities from the Tear Sheets in Chapter One will be used
to create appropriate electronic responses to the situation described in Student
Activities in Chapter 2.

In the following chapter, we will explore effective writing tools that we can employ in our communications with others that will ensure the highest probability that communications are received as intended.

Chapter Two

Using Technology to Deliver the Message Successfully

Document Form

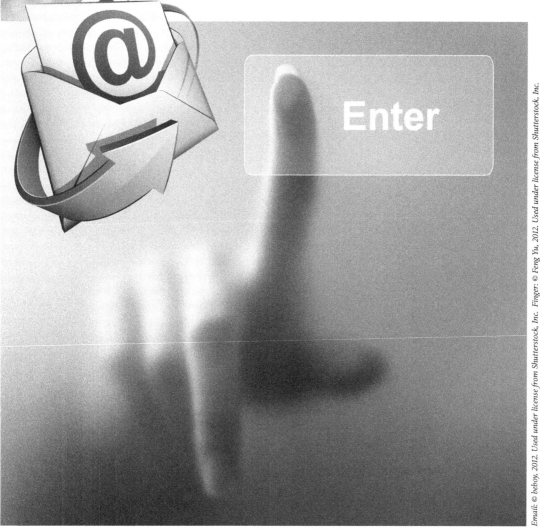

Chapter Two

Learning Objectives

LO1 Understand how expectation affects communication.

LO2 Describe how technology affects the communication process.

LO3 Describe current business document choices.

LO4 Describe current technologies used in business communication.

LO5 Identify the planning stages of writing.

LO6 Identify planning the communication according to document form.

LO7 Choose delivery given audience and objectives.

LO8 Understand current industry document formats, given document delivery choice

LO9 Compose an e-mail message, a text message, an instant message, a tweet, and a blog entry.

Intent Dictates Form and Expectation Affects Reception

The desired result of a communication determines communication form. From the most positive end of the spectrum, i.e., a promotion, job offer, or award, to the "negative news" end of the spectrum, such as announcing a layoff or a serious decline in company revenue, one needs to consider the reasons for the communication and its intended effect. The reasons for the communication set up the expectation for both the sender and the receiver. Expectation places the person in a particular frame of mind to receive the information in the communication. When the level of expectation is set appropriately, the receiver will accept the information more readily. Further, Lin in her study, "Sender-Receiver Framework for Knowledge Transfer," states "the sender and receiver form expectations of the value of knowledge based on their information" (Lin).

Coworker relationships develop and change with time, projects themselves evolve, the context of a business culture may change, and, generally, one's knowledge of the organization and mission become more comprehensive as one remains in a particular job role. That makes the decision making regarding the form that a communication should take become easier over time, as the knowledge set in many different aspects grows.

Taking into careful consideration the importance of setting the expectation appropriately so that the information exchange is valued and ultimately well received, helps determine what type of communication would be effective.

Technology and Communication

A very significant factor that affects our communications today is technology. It has provided us with a wide array of electronic tools for writing, producing reports, and presenting material.

Given the immediacy of communications involved with modern technology—in particular, the Internet—we often draft correspondence quickly without expecting it to be in good grammatical form. We have the intent of just delivering the message. Technology is fast and easy; we can text a message or e-mail without thinking too carefully about the content or form, then hit the "Send" button. Immediately, the message is sent and received. Sometimes that quick delivery can have undesired results.

Can you think of an instance when you sent a *message too quickly*? Perhaps the grammar was not formal enough for the person receiving the message. If you are sending a text or an e-mail to a college professor, you will probably want to make sure that it is grammatically correct. Yet you may have to create a mental shift in your mind to do that. Perhaps you spent more time that morning or afternoon casually texting to friends or family and using abbreviations such as "u" for "you" or "2" for "to," a few common texting acronyms. Consider that you may now be at work and have to send a more formal message or e-mail. Therefore, you need to be completely aware of spelling the words you abbreviated in your text, while omitting the emoticons. With fast technology, we are constantly shifting between informal and formal communications as we alternately use our smart phones for business as well as for personal communications.

In the workplace, often it is not only appropriate, but also common practice, to use e-mail. Yet, is it appropriate to send a text message to a fellow employee or a supervisor? Accepted practices in the business world are changing more quickly than ever now because of technology. It is very important to understand an organization's Acceptable Use Policies (AUPs). These regulate to a certain degree the communications of a business or a school. As technology changes, so do AUPs. Technology impacts the immediacy of the transfer of information as well. Many people are using smart phones that are capable of integrating applications, such as Web browsing, e-mail, texting, instant messaging (IM), and graphic capabilities. In fact, many organizations, both private and nonprofit, appreciate the immediacy of text messaging as leading to more spontaneous communications and efficiency.

Let us consider some common scenarios that are evolving because of technology. Not long ago, when phones were limited primarily to texting, a college professor would have been within reasonable expectations to post a sign that read "No Phones in the Classroom." Now, a college professor may see students accessing their online student database on their smart phones, including notes and directions for that class. Would they be within sensible or even practical parameters to ask those students not to use the smart phones in class? That same professor may have a guest speaker. A student might be taking notes on his cellular phone in silent mode while the speaker is presenting. Now the professor may have to think twice before asking that student not to use a phone in class. In a final scenario, a marketing professional attends a seminar on Google Analytics.™ She walks in the room to see every attendee with their laptops open on the table and their smart phones lying next to the computer while the speaker is presenting. In this case, the presenter's expectation is that attendees should bring their laptops and their smart phones, because there are critical information and online resources that will engage the attendees more effectively with the speaker and the topic.

Technology is changing quickly. As a result, acceptable use policies of organizations are changing as well. As a student or as an employee, it is important to know from the classroom to the conference room what the expectation of the arena is. In other words, what technologies are expected to be not just acceptable but used to a high degree of literacy? What computer, operating system, and application software does the company expect you to use and to what degree? How will we create, present, and publish reports? Now we see that it is not only the intended result that dictates the form of communication, and the expectations of the sender and the receiver, but also the availability of commonly used technologies that will play a role in dictating what type of message should be sent.

■ Mid-chapter Student Activity

 Using your favorite search engine, the keywords "Acceptable Use Policy," and the name of the organization or employer, find the accepted use policy (AUP) of your college or your employer, or another organization to which you belong. Compose a two paragraph Word document discussing your results. Name this file "AUP/student name."

Current Business Communication Forms

After considering the reason for the communication, the expectation level and knowledge sets of the individuals, and the existing technologies, one can decide on the form of the correspondence.

What communication form will you employ? Written and verbal are the two primary forms of communication in an organization. In this chapter, we will delve into written communication and its method of delivery. In subsequent chapters, we will examine techniques for effective public presentation deliveries.

Currently, companies are most often equipped with computers, and it would be difficult to imagine conducting business successfully without them. The Internet has made the world a smaller and more instantaneous environment, with the ability to receive instant responses, in real time, from business partners in remote parts of the world. Each of us can think about a friend, a family member, or a business partner we communicate with on a frequent basis, who is from another state or country.

In past practice, correspondence was sent via hard copy or traditional mail. This is referred to casually now as "snail mail." Company mail that remains inside the company is internal communication. Mail that goes outside the company, to a client or to a vendor, for example, is external communication. External communications are often more formal. However, internal communications such as those with financial or reporting data can be formal as well. Internal mail that is not in hard copy format is typically transmitted via e-mail on a computer network. An internal network is an intranet generally available only to employees or group members, whereas an external network goes beyond the company via the Internet.

E-mail is one of the most common forms of communication in an organization. If the e-mail contains significant informational content, then commonly an attachment is part of the e-mail as well. It is important to know how to send and receive e-mail with attachments, as well as to know how to download or save an attachment properly, or to prepare a document as an attachment for e-mail delivery.

Often, in addition to an e-mail address, business cards contain a company Web address or a Uniform Resource Locator (URL). as companies create that very important presence online. In fact, having a Website is now as common as a business card was several years ago. Web design itself, familiarity with Web design and use, and maintaining a strong Web presence are all expected skills in our modern business environment.

Further, given the abundance and the need for technology to conduct business, employees are expected to have a high degree of computer applications and Internet literacy. Social networking, where individuals exchange user generated content using the Web and mobile technologies, on sites such as Facebook, Twitter, LinkedIn, and many others, have grown exponentially over the past few years and are essential business tools that promote communication and increase marketing capability.

What is the common element with all of these technological tools and environments? The need to write is still the common thread! To communicate, to make your message heard, and to assure positive reception, with the intent to elicit ongoing good communication and good will, is still the most essential business ingredient. We express good will in writing and speaking through using a positive tone and avoiding words and messages that may offend. Good will is essential to adding value to a business beyond its tangible assets. Hardin (2009) discusses business practices that build good will and lead to the valuation of a company based on a loyal customer base and good practices among management and employees.

Business Communication Documents and Technologies

Internal Mail

Memos, letters, and company documents are internal company mail and sent via interoffice envelopes. Address these by simply placing the person's name and department on the envelope. If it is a confidential document, such as an evaluation, it should be marked "confidential" in either handwritten or stamped form. Documents in an internal mail package often are forms or reports in hard copy format and are procedural and substantial in nature. They often require a signature as well.

Manila Paper File Envelope close up

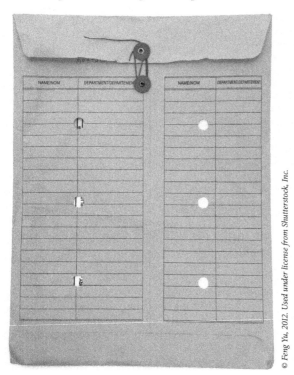

© Feng Yu, 2012. Used under license from Shutterstock, Inc.

FIGURE 1 *Traditional manila envelope.*

External Mail

Mail sent outside the company to a vendor, a client, or for service is usually more formal in nature and substantive as well. In a traditional mail format, the letter, request, bill, report, or memorandum is placed in an envelope and addressed to the recipient with the company's return address.

FIGURE 2 *Blank envelope. Isolated*

E-mail

E-mail is becoming the most common form of business communication and is used for both internal and external communications. It is common in business to have to sift through hundreds of e-mails daily, and to respond appropriately to them. This is a very time consuming endeavor. A common topic of conversation is if e-mail has increased employees' workloads. The Website IT Facts cites the Pew Internet Project, which shows that just 17% of Americans have an increase in their workload due to e-mail use (itfacts.biz, n.p.). In any case, this increased workload is keeping pace with technological changes and standards, which drive the tempo of the business culture on a local and global scale.

Several important considerations with e-mail involve the use of the carbon copy (cc) or blind carbon copy (bcc) functions, as well as the use of file attachments. The cc line on an e-mail is important as it includes other stakeholders in the conversation. There are some subtle considerations regarding the use of the cc line. Primary stakeholders, in position of their rank in the organizational hierarchy, should be placed in their respective orders on the "To" line; and, in the same fashion, subsidiary stakeholders should be placed in their respective hierarchical orders on the "cc" line. The "Blind Carbon Copy" (bcc) line is a function that allows the same document to be sent to many people, without e-mail addresses being visible to other members in the communication. This provides privacy and can be a legal consideration as well. A good example of the bcc would be a document that is shared with all students in a class. All students receive the document, but the recipient sees only the e-mail address of the sender, not the other "blind copy" recipients.

E-mail attachments

Attachments to the e-mail message may be saved in various formats. Often it is a Word or an Adobe Acrobat document that may contain hyperlinks to further information found on the Internet. If saved in the source document format, the file opens in the program that created it. In this case, the intent of the sender is that the receiver will be able to modify the document and then return the revised document to the sender. Sometimes, however, a message should be sent in a format that does not allow the receiver to alter the contents. On the whole, the most effective method is to save the document as a Portable Document Format (PDF) so that its contents cannot be easily modified. The ability to send and receive e-mails, to organize and manage them, and to upload and download attachments is essential, and it is an expected business proficiency.

Text messages

Short Message Service (SMS), commonly referred to as text messages, are an increasingly important and accepted means of communication in business. They are a relatively brief exchange of information sent via portable devices, with a maximum size of 160 characters (Figliola). The text message originated as a Short Message Service (SMS) and is the most widely used data application in the world, with 2.4 billion active users, or 74% of all mobile users (http://en.wikipedia.org/wiki/SMS). In Europe, it is referred to as SMS and in the Middle East and Asia it is TMS or SMS. Not only do companies text other employees and departments, text messages may be used, for example, officially to place important and time political votes in. Cellular (cell) phones are also used for safety purposes. In the event of a bomb threat or a criminal attack, company databases now have the ability to deliver text messages to students or employees, alerting them to potential terrorists or shooters on the premises. They are even used to alert residents of weather conditions. For instance, the New Jersey Alert text messaging system at www.njalert.gov (Cuyler) is used to alert residents to flood conditions.

Bulk SMS

Bulk Short Message Service (SMS) is becoming increasingly popular as a means to send hundreds if not thousands of messages. Its purposes are as far ranging as marketing to political campaigns to tracking health care outbreaks. In Zambia, health care workers were incentivized to use text messaging to send in results of rapid transmission diagnostics for malaria (MACEPA Path, Fighting Malaria Together Newsletter). The more rapidly the results were sent, the more free text minutes the health care workers received. Even a short message needs to be clearly and accurately written, if the intent is to reach hundreds or thousands of people, especially with a serious subject such as the example above regarding malaria transmission rates in Zambia.

Instant Messenger

Instant Messenger (IM) is a real time communication service between desktop computers. Users talk to each other while online at the same time, and they can send instantaneous text messages as well as small graphics. This form of communication is becoming increasingly popular in the business world and is a positive communication tool that is increasing office productivity. Scholars have been concerned about the use of IM in the workplace leading to interruptions and lower productivity. In fact, in their study on instant messaging and interruption in the workplace, Garret and Danziger (Garret, 2007) found that workers who use IM frequently on the job experienced less interruption than those who did not. Further, businesses are finding that in addition to IM use leading to increased productivity, there are additional benefits that businesses are experiencing as a result.

Twitter

Twitter is an online social networking and micro-blogging service that allows users to send and read text-based posts of up to 140 characters. Individuals, companies, politicians, and actors sign up for accounts that allow them to "follow" or "be followed" by other Twitter users. They post messages called "tweets." As "tweets" are posted, followers can read these short snippets of business and personal news, requests and offers for services and business deals. One can find numerous articles on the Internet regarding how to use Twitter for business, with hundreds of ideas regarding how this tweeting presence increases business contacts and deals.

Blogs

Another form of communication is a Blog, which is short for Web Log, and is something like an online diary, where people can post updates, and where topics range from personal interest and hobbies to causes and promotions. Others can comment on their "posts," which are usually in chronological order. As with most Internet sites, one needs to create a login profile with a username and a password. Initial use is free, but when one adds additional services, there are prorated fees. Businesses also use blogs to highlight their expertise, knowledge, products, and services. WordPress.com is one of the most popular blogging sites. In addition to being an excellent place to share information, "blogging" is an excellent way to practice writing skills.

We can note that as new communication technologies evolve, the length of the communication becomes shorter. E-mail can be lengthy, but it is usually less than a page in length; text messages are limited to 160 characters, instant messages are usually no more than a few lines in length, and tweets are limited to 140 characters. Additionally, text messaging and instant messaging abbreviate language. There are text messaging and chat dictionaries that can be easily found online that contain abbreviated words, acronyms specifically for texting, as well as emoticons, which are graphic symbols used to show emotion, i.e., the very common "smiley face" emoticon. ☺

Computer mediated communication is a term for a form of communication between individuals that has evolved as a result of the Internet and other network sharing environments. There are many theories and emerging studies regarding the impact of text messaging on language and communication. In one study, David Jacobson (Jacobson) examined instant messaging or text messaging as a form of computer mediated communication that posits that different meanings

FIGURE 3 *The traditional method of sending messages using envelopes, now referred to as "snail mail"*

are associated with the same message in different contexts. Context is an important factor to keep in mind, even in these shorter communications. Due to the rapidly changing nature of technologies, computer mediated communication is a field of study that is abundant with newly evolving studies and theories.

However, in spite of the medium used, it is essential that writing be concise and effective. Excellent communication skills are critical to securing and holding a job, as well as rising to the level and position that you desire within an organization. After all, consider the end result. Better writing and speaking net more profit and lead to effective communication, team building, and good will, all factors that lead to engaged employees and successful organizational results.

FIGURE 4 *E-mail, one of the most common forms of electronic business communication*

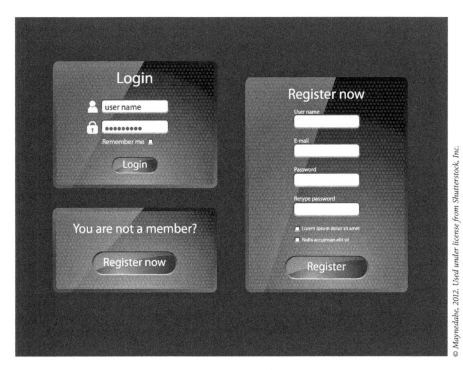

FIGURE 5 *Social Networking, keeping pace with e-mail and texting*

FIGURE 6 *Text messaging is very widely used in business and for personal communications.*

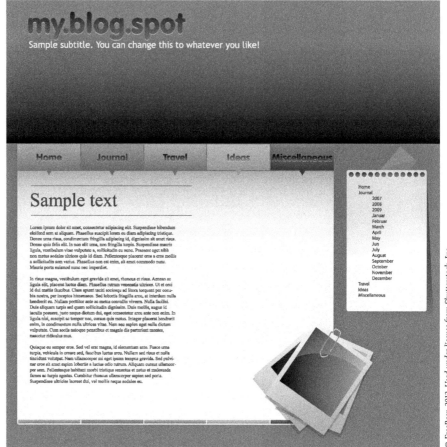

FIGURE 7 *Blogs have various backgrounds, images, and layouts.*

The first stage of the three-step writing process, "planning, composing and revising," is planning. This involves critically thinking about the purpose and content of the message, as well as the intended audience, before you start composing it. The next step of the writing process is original composition. This is the lengthiest stage of the writing process. As discussed previously, this stage should involve a draft and, if complex, an outline. Finally, the revision process is important to fine-tune the writing. It assures that the writing is organized, contains transitions, avoids common grammatical errors, and is concise. Furthermore, this stage is your final chance to adjust the tone, to make the writing come alive, and to consider how the final copy will meet the initial objective of the correspondence. It is also important in this stage to anticipate your recipient's perception of the final copy.

Planning

Consider the following when in the planning stages of writing.

- Intent, need or objective
- Length of communication and allocation of time based on length
- Format of the document, i.e., memorandum, e-mail, business letter, or report
- Use of a rough draft
- Use of an outline
- Audience and level of formality or informality in the relationship(s)
- Content: factual, common, or organizational
- Reporting order for carbon copies and blind carbon copies

Remember that effective business communication occurs when the purpose of the sender meets the needs of the receiver. The writer's intent and the recipient's needs should be the first item of deliberation. As discussed in previous chapters, you need to be aware of the intent of the communication. What is the objective or reason for the communication? Additionally, have you considered the intended outcome? Do you need to send a quick e-mail to confirm a meeting? Alternatively, do you need to send a more lengthy invitation for a meeting? How will you respond to a dissatisfied client? Will the e-mail contain factual data in a report format, in attachment format?

The length of the document can be determined based on the purpose of the writer. Length determines the amount of time you will need to dedicate to the process. If the document is lengthy, it may involve writing a rough draft of the document, then revising the document several times before sending. If you can allow the time to look at more lengthy documents and communications a second or third time, it is well worth the time and effort.

If an attachment is required, then you may need to prepare factual data, to check its veracity, and to prepare it in the proper format. Establish the objective, and then consider your audience and stakeholders. If you are sending an e-mail, who is on the primary "To" line? Do you need to send copies and, if so, as carbon copies with names on the "Cc" line in order of the company-reporting chart, or on the "Bcc" line? In addition, will you send the communication electronically or via traditional mail?

The level of formality and informality of the stakeholders is another one of our primary considerations to determine communication form. On one end of the spectrum, if you are inviting industry members to your advisory meeting, you will want to be structured and formal, even if you have met with those persons outside of the business arena. However, if you work closely with a colleague and have frequent daily communications with the person, the writing might take a more casual form. In past standard business letter format, the familiarity of the relationship dictated the use of a colon for a more formal relationship or a comma for a more casual one. You should adhere to this standard in present business correspondence, even with more casual e-mail communications.

The Planning Process According to Document Form

Document form once decided upon will then dictate factors involved in the planning process. In this section, we will discuss in detail pertinent factors involved with each of the correspondences discussed in Chapter Two, in the order of their common use and length. In addition, you will see examples of document formatting, according to standard business format, including current technologies for communications. It is important to have visuals of the format, length, and layout of a document while in the planning stages of writing.

Standard Hard Copy Business Documents

Standard business letters, composed on a word processor, printed on letterhead stationery, and signed, still have a place in today's modern business world. Examples of when you need to send this type of correspondence include a signed contract, a letter of recommendation, or a formal bid for a project or proposal.

Examples of standard business letters abound on the Internet, and are in Microsoft Word templates, where you can modify a template to suit your own needs. They also exist on many college or university Websites, and of course in business textbooks. It is critical in the planning stages to know the accepted business format of the documents that you are going to prepare. To that end, we will practice searching for and formatting various business documents before focusing on their content.

■ **Student Activities Mid chapter Check point**

 Chapter 3, Student Activity One: Open Microsoft Word; go to File, New to locate the template section. Use the keywords "contract" for your first search, "letter of recommendation" for your second search, and "proposal" for your third search. Download the documents one by one and save them with the same file names you used for your search "contract," "letter of recommendation," and "proposal." Add your name, i.e., "letter of recommendation_student_name" where your name replaces "student name."

 Chapter 3, Student Activity One, A. Remember to use this structure when writing for this short comparative/contrast exercise:
- 1, 3, 5 rule
- One opening or topic sentence for each paragraph
- Introduction (3 lines)
- Supporting paragraph one: (5 sentences). For this assignment, similarities
- Supporting paragraph two: (5 sentences). For this assignment, differences
- Concluding paragraph (3 lines)
- Remember to turn on Spelling AND Grammar! Edit three times!!!

What are the common elements that you have found in the three documents that you chose? What elements are different? What is the format of the document? Is it single spaced, double-spaced? Do you think the format of a formal standard business letter is an important consideration?

Chapter 3, Student Activity Two: Using your favorite search engine, use keywords "Block Style Business Letter guidelines, university" to find sample business letters and writing guides that you consider to be a good search result. Copy and paste the URL (Web address) of that site into your activity and discuss the information that you found on that Website in a two-three paragraph response. Include specific examples of business letters and/or practices that you find interesting or helpful.

Basic Business Letters

Block Style Block style hard copy letters should be written if a signature is required and in more formal circumstances. All text is left-aligned in a modified block style letter.

To apply standard business letter formatting properly in Word 2016, you will need to change a few Microsoft settings. This involves a) clearing text of any existing formatting, as, for example, in a template, b) changing the default line spacing from 1.15 to 1, and c) removing the spacing after paragraphs.

To do this:

1. In the Font Group, choose Clear Formatting
2. In the Paragraph Group, choose 1.0 (single spacing)
3. In the Paragraph Group, choose Remove Space After Paragraph

The procedure above allows the line spacing to return to a normal single spacing, with no extra space before or after the return, and with no other formatting applied.

Font choice in relation to readability is another consideration when formatting a business document. The most widely accepted font for the Web or in electronic documents for the body of the document is Verdana, 10 point, due to its san serif format and larger spacing between characters. In smaller areas of the document, use Arial 10 point font as it is also a sans serif font, but the spacing is smaller between characters (a3webtech.com). For printed text, the most commonly used font for readability is still Times New Roman, 12-point font.

Another consideration is often uncertainty regarding the use of one or two spaces between the state and the zip code in an address. According to the postal addressing standards issued by the government, "two spaces are preferred between the state abbreviation and ZIP+4 code" (Postal Addressing Standards 2).

Current Date

Title, First Name, Last Name
Company Name
City, State Zip Code

Recipient Title, First Name, Last Name
Company Name
City, State Zip Code

Dear Title Last Name:

Capture the attention of the reader in this opening paragraph! Start with a strong opening sentence. Paragraph one is the introductory paragraph and it is the first paragraph the recipient will read, so it is very important, just like first impressions. Here you introduce the recipient to your reason for sending the correspondence and summarize what you are going to address.

Paragraph two should be the longest paragraph because it should contain the ideas that you introduced in paragraph one, but with supporting examples and detail. Pay attention to the order of informational items. Bring the topics up in paragraph two in the order that you introduced them in paragraph one. State the topic or assertion, and then follow with a supporting example. Conclude paragraph two with a nice transitional line that flows into paragraph three.

This concluding paragraph typically thanks the recipient for taking the time to review the information carefully, and then asks for action by stating that you are looking forward to meeting them or hearing from them soon.

Closing,

Title, First Name, Last Name
Company Name

Typist's initials, lower case

BLOCK STYLE BUSINESS LETTER TEMPLATE

FIGURE 1 *Block Style Business Letter Template*

Current Date¶

Title, First Name, Last Name¶
Company Name¶
City, State Zip Code¶

Recipient Title, First Name, Last Name¶
Company Name¶
City, State Zip Code¶

Dear Title Last Name:¶

Capture the attention of the reader in this opening paragraph! Start with a strong opening sentence. Paragraph one is the introductory paragraph and it is the first paragraph the recipient will read, so it is very important, just like first impressions. Here you introduce the recipient to your reason for sending the correspondence and summarize what you are going to address.¶

Paragraph two should be the longest paragraph, because it should contain the ideas that you introduced in paragraph one, but with supporting examples and with detail. Pay attention to the order of informational items. Bring the topics up in paragraph two in the order that you introduced them in paragraph one. State the topic or assertion, and then follow with a supporting example. Conclude paragraph two with a nice transitional line that flows into paragraph three.¶

This concluding paragraph typically thanks the recipient for taking the time to review the information carefully, and then asks for action by stating that you are looking forward to meeting them or hearing from them soon.¶

Closing,¶

Title, First Name, Last Name¶
Company Name¶

Typist's initials, lower case¶

BLOCK STYLE BUSINESS LETTER TEMPLATE¶
Note spacing indicated by paragraph return symbols¶

FIGURE 2 *Block Style Business Letter Template*

January 13, 2017

Jackie Martin
President
Business Writing With An Edge
7317 Precipice Place
Bridge, CA 11897

Ms. Jane Doe
Marketing Director
Writing for Success
Success Drive
Madyson County, KS 92345

Dear Ms. Doe,

We are pleased to inform you that our Marketing and Sales Director, the CFO, and investors accepted your business Plan for the new internet startup company "Writing for Success." The next step would be to meet the team!

We will hold the meeting in our Conference Room, #D11, and provide you with an overhead projector, a laptop, and white board. Our AV department will set up the connections and make sure that all is working well technically. Your presentation should not exceed thirty minutes. Refreshments will be served during a period of open dialog after the presentation. Please plan to arrive 30 minutes early to ensure that all is working properly. If you have other equipment needs or suggestions for the meeting, please respond directly to this email.

Finally, please RSVP Mr. Titus, Assistant to the V.P., with your most convenient day and time for this meeting. We are looking forward to meeting you and to collaborating with you in this partner venture.

Sincerely,

Jackie Martin
President

kh

FIGURE 3 *Block Style Business Letter With Sample Text.*

Another consideration in standard business letter formatting is the margin setting. Regarding margins, use one inch standard margins for all business letters.

Modified Block Style Business Letter

A modified block style letter is another style of standard business letter, which is identical to the block style letter, except that the date and signature line are indented seven tab stops to the right. Therefore, following the example of the block letter in the previous section, everything remains the same except the date and signature line.

■ **Spacing Considerations with Block and Modified Block Style Letters:**
It is helpful when determining the spacing of the document (single or double), to use a feature in Word called "Show/Hide," which shows hidden formatting symbols, including the paragraph return mark. See the illustration below.

Basic Business Memorandums

A business memorandum (memo) is usually sent as an internal document to accomplish some task within the organization. If it is sent as an external hard copy document, it still contains the traditional memo block and a signature does not follow the memo body.

To:
From:
Date:
Subject:

Memorandum Block

The memo is typically shorter than a block or a modified block letter, and the format is somewhat different. A common form of correspondence is the e-mail memo. The e-mail itself has transformed the memo block shown above, with the "To," "From," "Date," and "Subject" lines converted to the "To," "From," "Cc," "Bcc," and "Subject" lines, and the date is literally stamped in real time when the e-mail is sent. Additionally, though there is a "To" line in the electronic or e-mail memo, the sender's name and title are expected to appear at the bottom of the memo, unlike in a hard copy memo. The example below illustrates the differences between a hard copy traditional memo and an e-mail memo.

Single or double space paragraphs, include greeting and closing lines.

TO: JaneDoe@abc.net

FROM: jmartin@123.net

Cc: pertinentparty@456.net, 2ndpertinentparty@456.net

Bcc: hrmanager@123.net

SUBJECT: Short and Concise Main Subject Line

Dear Title Last Name:

Capture the attention of the reader in this opening paragraph! Start with a strong opening sentence. Paragraph one is the introductory paragraph and it is the first paragraph the recipient will read, so it is very important, just like first impressions. Here you introduce the recipient to your reason for sending the correspondence and summarize what you are going to address.

Paragraph two should be the longest paragraph, because it should contain the ideas that you introduced in paragraph one, but with supporting examples and with detail. Pay attention to the order of informational items. Bring the topics up in paragraph two in the order that you introduced them in paragraph one. State the topic or assertion, and then follow with a supporting example. Conclude paragraph two with a nice transitional line that flows into paragraph three.

This concluding paragraph typically thanks the recipient for taking the time to review the information carefully, and then asks for action by stating that you are looking forward to meeting them or hearing from them soon.

Closing,

Title, First Name, Last Name
Company Name
Phone, extension

Typist's initials, lower case

E-MAIL MEMORANDUM TEMPLATE
Single or double space paragraphs, include Greeting and Closing Lines

FIGURE 4 *E-Mail Memorandum Template.*

January 13, 2017

Jackie Martin
President
Business Writing With An Edge
7317 Precipice Place
Bridge, CA 11897

Ms. Jane Doe
Marketing Director
Writing for Success
Success Drive
Madyson County, KS 92345

Dear Ms. Doe,

We are pleased to inform you that our Marketing and Sales Director, the CFO, and investors accepted your business Plan for the new internet startup company "Writing for Success." The next step would be to meet the team!

We will hold the meeting in our Conference Room, #D11, and provide you with an overhead projector, a laptop, and white board. Our AV department will set up the connections and make sure that all is working well technically. Your presentation should not exceed thirty minutes. Refreshments will be served during a period of open dialog after the presentation. Please plan to arrive 30 minutes early to ensure that all is working properly. If you have other equipment needs or suggestions for the meeting, please respond directly to this email.

Finally, please RSVP Mr. Titus, Assistant to the V.P., with your most convenient day and time for this meeting. We are looking forward to meeting you and to collaborating with you in this partner venture.

Sincerely,

Jackie Martin
President

kh

FIGURE 5 *Modified Block Style Business Letter With Sample Text.*

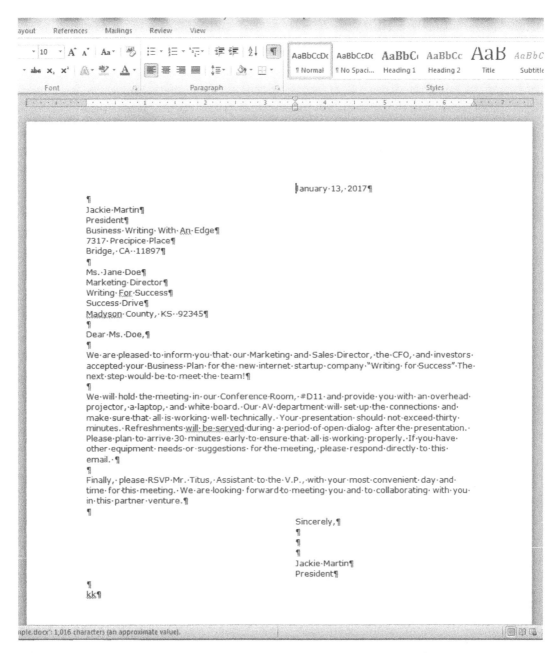

FIGURE 6 *Modified Block Style Business Letter Showing Use of Enter Key for Spacing*

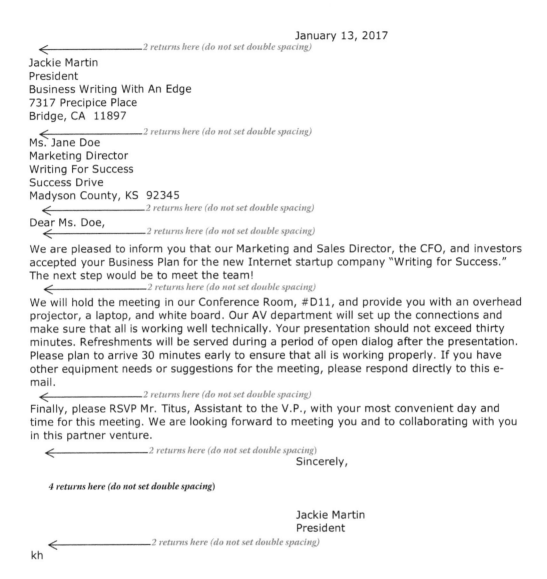

FIGURE 7 *Modified Block Style Business Letter Showing Line Spacing.*

Composing an Electronic or E-mail Document

If an e-mail contains significant information, such as a procedure or a response to lengthy informational requests, it is a good idea to compose it in a word processing program first offline. Revise and spell-check, put it down for a few hours if deadlines allow, then revise it again after your mind has had the chance to distance itself from the comprehension. Finally, copy and paste the information into the e-mail message when you are certain it is in good form.

However, if the e-mail is short and a quick response, then you can compose online directly in the e-mail body, but keep a few important things in mind. Make sure you are using proper grammar, that you are neither too formal nor informal given the recipient and the subject matter, and use the spellchecker before sending. Before hitting the "Send" button, read the message one more time and envision the audience. If it is sensitive in nature, you may want to have a trusted colleague or friend read the letter first.

E-mail Attachments

Often e-mail messages need supporting documentation. If this is the case, an e-mail may have an attachment(s) that can be opened by the recipient. If the intent is to change the document, then it can be sent in its original or native format. However, if it is simply meant to be read, and not changed, we call this "read only," and it is sent in a popular format called Portable Document Format or PDF. A feature called "insert" or "attach" accompanied by a paper clip is the most common command found to "attach" the document(s) to the e-mail.

Text Messages

Text messages are short and often abbreviated, as they are limited to approximately 160 characters. Therefore, many text messages as well as instant messages contain abbreviations. There are many online sites that have complete dictionaries of abbreviations used in chat rooms and when writing short messaging. The most important factor regarding text messaging should be to ensure that there is enough text to convey the intended message.

© iofoto, 2012. Used under license from Shutterstock, Inc.

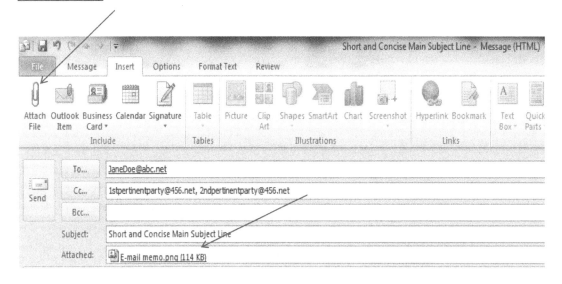

Dear Title Last Name:

Capture the attention of the reader in this opening paragraph! Start with a strong opening sentence. Paragraph one is the introductory paragraph and it is the first paragraph the recipient will read, so it is very important, just like first impressions. Here you introduce the recipient to your reason for sending the correspondence and summarize what you are going to address.

Paragraph two should be the longest paragraph, because it should contain the ideas that you introduced in paragraph one, but with supporting examples and with detail. Pay attention to the order of informational items. Bring the topics up in paragraph two in the order that you introduced them in paragraph one. State the topic or assertion, and then follow with a supporting example. Conclude paragraph two with a nice transitional line that flows into paragraph three.

This concluding paragraph typically thanks the recipient for taking the time to review the information carefully, and then asks for action by stating that you are looking forward to meeting them or hearing from them soon.

Closing,

Title, First Name, Last Name
Company Name
Phone, extension

Typist's initials, lower case

FIGURE 8 *E-Mail Memorandum with File Attachment*

In other words, do not "over abbreviate" and make sure the message is formal or informal enough to be appropriate for the situation. Additionally, people often feel a degree of false distance and bravado when writing or texting, so be careful that what you write is what you would feel comfortable saying directly to the friend, family member, or coworker to whom you are writing.

■ Mid-chapter Student Activity

 Chapter Three, Student Activity Four: Find a text-messaging dictionary online and compose a text message using a balance of words, phrases, and abbreviations that gets the message across.

Bulk SMS or Bulk Text Messages

Bulk Text Messages or Bulk SMS is a form of communication that is rapidly catching on in the business environment. When a merchant makes a purchase and volunteers to give the store her cell phone number, that number becomes part of a database that is used to send marketing messages to many merchants, via their cell phones. It is a new form of marketing that can reach hundreds or even thousands of people with very up to date and succinct text messages. The same principles should apply to writing techniques for bulk MSM as for a single text message, except that it should be very clear and the writing style should be business appropriate.

 Chapter Three, Student Activity Five: How would one obtain cell phone numbers given the private status of those numbers? A company or organization must have collected the numbers and data on their customers, or those they serve, to have a contact list.

 Chapter Three, Student Activity Six: Can you find an occurrence of bulk text messages being sent in an emergency? Examples might include a campus shooter, an impending threatening storm or tornado, or other sudden crisis.

Instant Messaging (IM)

Instant messaging is also a form of communication that occurs in real time through an online site with users who have IM accounts. The benefits of IM'ing are that you are typing in real time, and that you can choose the recipient, unlike chat rooms where anyone in a particular group can log on. Often, there is an IM feature associated with a user's e-mail account. Instant Messaging is becoming accepted as a viable and expedient form of business communication.

© Stocklite, 2012. Used under license from Shutterstock, Inc.

Tweets

If you are wondering why text messages are limited to 160 characters, Ogaswara (Ogaswara, 2012) from the Social Times, helps us answer that question. He points to an article in *The New York Times* that discusses research Friedhelm Hillebrand, (Milian, 2009), working for German Telecom, conducted. He performed some simple tests by typing random sentences and questions on a sheet of paper. The combination of characters—including letters, numbers, spaces, and punctuation, nearly always clocked in at fewer than 160 characters. This "magic number" thus set the standard to standardize cell phone technology communication.

Just as with text messages, tweets are short and concise, and they use abbreviations to deliver the message. The difference between the two is that we send text messages via cell phones or smartphones, and we post tweets to an online site called Twitter, with a unique account that you set up with your unique username and password.

© Annette Shaff, 2012. Used under license from Shutterstock, Inc.

Blogs

As discussed in Chapter 2, a blog stands for Web log and is an online "diary" that can be used to write a post about any topic, ranging from personal to business interests. Blogs support text, graphics, and hyperlinks and can be commented on by users and viewers. Blogs allow people to share their writing, opinions, and knowledge to the world via online postings. A user creates an account, and can administer that account as well. There are many engaging blog sites online that illustrate interesting content, hobbies, and art.

In addition to the document formats discussed above, the structure of the organization, as well as the context of the need for that communication, dictate the form. For example, if we are in a more formal organizational structure, with clearly defined lines of responsibility, there is most likely a company form, or protocol, that you can access via the company Website. Employees are expected to adhere to the use of these forms and protocols. As a new employee, it takes time to acquaint oneself with the proper forms to use for monthly, quarterly, or yearly reports, but it is important to get familiar with these forms as quickly as possible to "fit" within the norms of the company culture and expectations. There is a grace period during which one is given time to learn, but, eventually, one is expected to use the proper form for a given procedure. The company's Website typically will have links to the forms and procedures of that company.

In conclusion, we have examined common business documents and their various formats. Once we have decided upon the business communication format, whether memo, text, tweet, or email, we can focus on composition including content, style, and tone.

Student Activity Pages

 We will be using our case study from Chapter One. Online Classroom Site Assignment Link Chapter Two, #2.

Scenario (Use the same case study throughout the book so that the same documents can be edited repetitively and adapted to different scenarios in chapters.)

> Mr. Smith, Sales Director
> Ms. Malloy, Marketing Director
> Mr. Ruiz, Marketing & Sales Manager
> Company: Business Writing With An Edge Consulting Group

■ Situation

Mr. Smith and Ms. Malloy have been coworkers for several years, working closely together. Over the past year, Mr. Smith and Ms. Malloy have engaged in a more personal relationship. Apparently, the relationship is not working out, so Ms. Malloy would like Mr. Smith to stop communicating with her through company e-mail. Mr. Smith does not want to end the relationship so continues to send her personal e-mails, even after Ms. Malloy has asked him several times to stop.

As Mr. Smith continues, Ms. Malloy finally tires of this behavior and writes an e-mail memo to her supervisor, Mr. Ruiz, who also is Mr. Smith's supervisor. She threatens to sue the company if Mr. Smith does not stop corresponding with her using company e-mail. She states that she can no longer work closely with Mr. Smith and feels that his behavior will negatively affect the marketing campaign that they have been working on for over a year.

Mr. Ruiz decides to call a meeting with Mr. Smith alone first.

Discussion Considerations Should work e-mail be used for personal correspondence? To whom should Ms. Malloy have sent the e-mail? To whom should she not have sent the correspondence? What was her aim, her audience, her goal? What form of communication should she have used?

■ Notes to instructor

Feedback from Ms. Malloy's supervisor was negative, so should she use that to gauge future communication and change her behavior? Ms. Malloy should realize she implicated herself by using company e-mail. She can improve by not using company e-mail, by having private conversations, and by involving HR if Mr. Smith is harassing. In addition, perhaps Ms. Malloy should have had a spoken conversation first with her supervisor, without using a threat of escalation.

■ Action

Work in your assigned group. Each group member should use Word or another word processing program to write the following communications. Spellcheck your document thoroughly and review it.

Read one another's work. Choose the best document in each group and choose someone to read the document to the rest of the class, using an LCD presentation system.

■ Note to instructor and students

If students have access to computers in the classroom, ideally you can use an LCD presentation system to show the "chosen" document to the class. Students should save their work to a USB drive that can be plugged into the instructor computer station and displayed to the class. If the classroom is loaded with Synchronize™, the instructor can control the students' computers and "share" the document then edit the document line by line with the class. This is a terrifically successful way to edit a document. Students are very engaged and learn from others' excellent writing as well as from their mistakes. Without an LCD, you may use a traditional overhead projector to display a printed copy of the document. Students can take notes on the edits suggested by the class and one student can edit the document electronically as the class is making suggestions and receiving approvals from the instructor.

Refer to your handwritten notes in the "SIX-STEP TRANSFORMATIONAL COMMUNICATION CYCLE ACTIVITY TABLE" and the "communication cycle activity table" from Chapter 2 to compose the following documents.

Also, take into consideration the recipient's information set. What is the level of shared knowledge? Remember, valued and well-received information relies on a complete information set. Also, consider the formality of the company as well as the relationship of the employees. Finally, the length of the communication should be appropriate.

Compose the following documents:

1. An initial e-mail message, from Ms. Malloy to Mr. Ruiz, threatening to sue the company if Mr. Smith does not cease personal correspondence through company e-mail. (no more than one half page)
2. An e-mail message in response to the e-mail in Step 1 above, written by Mr. Ruiz. You determine who the recipients of this e-mail should be, and what lines the e-mail should be on (cc line and/or bcc line). Also, decide if there should be any additional recipients, for example, the Human Resources Department.
3. A text message, from Ms. Malloy to Mr. Smith, reminding him that she does not want to receive further communication (maximum 160 characters)
4. An instant message (IM) from Mr. Ruiz to Mr. Smith stating that he would like to see him as soon as his schedule permits. (maximum two or three short sentences)
5. A tweet from Ms. Malloy on her Twitter site, discussing her day at work. You decide the appropriate content.
6. A reflective Web blog entry titled "Ms. Malloy's Memo Chapter Two Entry" using your classroom blog: per your instructor's directions in response to the situation with Mr. Smith, Ms. Malloy and Mr. Ruiz. Remember, this is a public forum, so follow proper blogging etiquette. It should be two paragraphs in length, and be a reflective but positive piece of writing by Ms. Malloy.
7. According to your instructor's directions, zip all files from activities 1 to 6 above. Name each one of the files according to the step number (1, 2, etc.) i.e., "Step 1_Student_Name" and upload to your Online Classroom Site or as instructed.

Composition: Sentence, Paragraph and Whole Document Considerations

Chapter Three

Learning Objectives

LO1 Describe the importance of adaptation in business writing composition.

LO2 Build clear and concise sentences, paragraphs, and documents.

LO3 Build paragraphs with proper content, style, and transitions.

LO4 Compose entire documents with proper style.

LO5 Identify slang and discriminatory language.

LO6 Identify and use the active voice in writing.

LO7 Identify clichés and idioms.

LO8 Identify best practices in sentence design.

LO9 Compose sentences using best practices.

LO10 Describe the importance of revision to promote change in communication.

I n this chapter, we will be focusing on step 2 of the writing process, composing our message so that both sender and receiver can process information in a similar fashion. After determining the reason for the communication, the expectation level, and the form, you can begin the writing process. We live in an Information Age where technology is our primary tool for composing and delivering a good message. However, the thought, preparation, structure, and actual writing still take place in our minds and we deliver it through the writing process.

The message, whether written or spoken, delivered through pencil and paper or via technology has to be well written and concise. Furthermore, it is highly desirable to have the recipient receive the message according to its intent. To that end, it is important that both sender and receiver are working within a similar context and tone and have a similar knowledge base within which to interpret the message. We will consider these factors and more as we move into our discussion of composing the message. As we progress from word choice, to sentence structure, then to paragraph structure, and finally to whole document considerations, we will also practice writing techniques for neutral messages, positive messages, negative or "bad news" messages, and finally persuasive messages and proposals.

Composition

You create an outline in the planning stage of the writing process. Now you are ready to write the full document. Many people in this stage of the writing process face what is referred to as "writer's block." The task of writing on a "blank page" is daunting. Furthermore, the writing process originates from a thinking process, and thoughts can be brilliant and plentiful, but random and not precise in their first expression. Therefore, it is helpful to use writing aides such as outlines, and examples of well-written documents. It is also helpful, especially in the business arena, to know what classifications of documents to use and then choose appropriately given the situation. Once the writing process begins, it is important to keep the writing of the first draft moving forward. You can use an outline, break the content down into chunks, motivate yourself with a reward after writing a certain number of paragraphs, and compare the original document to the finished product to see how much more refined and clear the writing is in the final stages. It is also very helpful to put the document down to break comprehension, then take a second and third look at the document to revise it with "fresh eyes." Polishing a piece of writing is like polishing a wooden carving. They each become less rough, smoother, and more refined with each finishing process.

Audience and Adaptation

A few general considerations regardless of the type of message should be deliberated first. Knowing the audience is an important factor as it relates to the ability to adapt the message to the intended audience. Age, sex, and cultural considerations are all part of this decision making process. If you are creating materials for a presentation in Japan, with executives or technical people who know your product intimately and have the same level of expertise, then you can be technical and speak that industry jargon. However, if your product is robotics and you are conducting an outreach campaign as the company liaison to an elementary school, then gear your materials and presentation to a young audience. You will have to adapt your presentations using words that young students will understand and

marketing messages that appeal to that younger audience. Ask yourself, what is the level of formality in the relationship? Is this a formal letter, as would be sent to an external client? Is it a message to a peer on the hierarchical chain of command in the organization, therefore lending informality? Or are you writing to a supervisor, in which case the tone should be more formal. Keep these overarching considerations in mind for all messages.

Building Concise and Clear Sentences

Word Choice Our end goal in producing writing that is crisp, concise, and effective requires that we choose our words carefully. In addition to writing with clarity, selecting appropriate words involves being mindful of avoiding language that is too familiar, which may be used in everyday casual conversation, as well as the use of slang and possible discriminatory language.

Slang Slang is very informal language and is inappropriate for formal writing. It is language used by a particular group of people; it can be defined by age, geographic locations, and cultural backgrounds; and it is short-lived as well. Within a few years, the slang that is popular now will be outdated. Therefore, you should avoid it in written and oral communications in business. You might want to greet your friend by saying, "What's up?" or concur with a friend about the latest movie you liked: "Sweet!" However, you most likely would not want to greet your boss or your mother or father with the same "What's up?" The use of slang can also create exclusion. Those who are not part of that particular social group may not even understand it. In fact, the use of these examples of slang in subsequent versions of this text will even become outdated!

Discriminatory Language One of the most offensive and unacceptable forms of language—discriminatory or derogatory language—reinforces stereotypes based on factors such as age, race, political and religious beliefs, or sexual orientation. Just as with slang, people may feel excluded based on these discriminatory language references, and even abused in extreme cases. Modern society does not tolerate this type of language and even has very well established policies in the workplace to prohibit it. Furthermore, you need to be extremely careful with references that you may think are acceptable even in a casual conversation in the workplace or in the telling of a story, joke, or casual "water cooler" conversation, because individuals may be very sensitive to these issues.

How can we avoid the cluttering and negative effects of slang? Practice these principles:

1. Write more formally than you speak.

2. Eliminate slang and discriminatory words from your writing entirely.

3. Put yourself in the other's shoes—use a "you" point of view.

4. Analyze your writing.

Discriminatory language targeted at various groups or individuals can take various forms. Derogatory labeling, depersonalizing, making jokes, stereotyping, and creating invisibility are all examples of exclusive language use and each has its own nuances. It is limiting, creates a negative categorization for a particular group, depersonalizes people, and makes them invisible.

Labeling is often targeted at people with disabilities or different sexual orientations.

Offensive terms used to refer to persons with disabilities include:

■ Crippled

■ Deaf and dumb

■ Retarded

These terms are euphemisms that came into being because there is often discomfort or embarrassment surrounding people who are not fully capable of functioning in life and work.

Instead, use these positive terms:

■ Person(s) with disabilities

■ Colleague(s) or coworker with disabilities

■ Brother or sister with a disability

By making the individual, rather than the disability, the main subject, you avoid equating the person with the disability. Instead, you are now acknowledging and respecting the individual as a member of a work group, an organization, or a family unit. If you need to name the disability, simply add "person with," or "person has," "person living with," or something similar in front of the name of the disability or condition.

Therefore, the examples above extend this way:

- Person with epilepsy

- Colleague with Downs Syndrome

- Brother or sister who lives with mental illness

Sexual orientation also causes a degree of discomfort in people and is one of the last forms of discrimination to be addressed. Fortunately, civil rights groups, activists, politicians, and others in support of the cause have made great strides in recent years to assure equal treatment for all, regardless of sexual orientation. In December 2011, in front of the United Nations, Secretary of State Hillary Clinton (Bennett, 2011) delivered a historic LGBT Speech in Geneva declaring that "Gay Rights Are Human Rights." She acknowledged the history of that discrimination, and addressed the progress our country has made towards bringing to light an often oppressed, abused, and excluded group of citizens.

Terms used to define an individual's sexual orientation have changed over the years, and what is acceptable in one context may not be in another. In the LGBTQ (Lesbian, Gay, Bisexual, Transgender, and Queer) community, the term used may even imply a certain political outlook. Again, euphemisms such as "batting for the other team" or "that way" are pejorative and often develop because of discomfort with a norm or standard that differs from one's own. Great care must be taken in business writing and business speech to dignify the rights of all human beings by choosing appropriate nondiscriminatory language.

Gender and Age Neutral Language Gender and age neutral word choices are also important considerations in business writing. People live longer, work longer, and retire later; therefore, the older worker is becoming a significant player in the work force. *The Christian Science Monitor* terms the older workers, age 55 and above, the "gray labor" force, and states that they will account for 90 percent of the labor market increase between 2008 and 2018 (Kaslow, 2011). One of the great changes in the past 50 years is the empowerment of women and their presence in the workforce. As of October 2009, women make up almost half of American workers (Economist.com) Given these changes in the makeup of the workforce, references in business messages should present these contingencies in a positive light, avoiding any kind of discriminatory language associated with age or gender. Further, historically in English writing and speech we have been schooled to use masculine nouns and pronouns. Gender-neutral language is language that avoids this masculine reference and is inclusive.

Seeing the examples of gender-biased and gender-neutral language side by side illustrates the point nicely.

Gender-Age Biased	Gender-Age Neutral (Use these!)
1. Actress	Actor, Performer
2. Anchorman	Anchor, Anchorperson
3. Businessman	Business Person, Executive
4. Chairman, Chairwoman	Chair
5. Cleaning Lady	Housekeeper
6. Congressman	Member of Congress, Representative
7. Councilman, Councilwoman	Council Member
8. Craftsman	Craftsperson, Artisan
9. Draftsman	Drafter, Drafting Technician
10. Young	Avoid any reference to age and instead speak of skills and abilities.
11. Energetic	Able to excel in fast-paced environment
12. Seasoned	Avoid any reference to age.
13.	
14.	
15.	
16.	
17.	
18.	
19.	
20.	
21.	
22.	
23.	
24.	
25.	
26.	
27.	
28.	
29.	
30.	

FIGURE 9

■ Mid-chapter Student Activity

 Complete the list by finding more gender-neutral and age-neutral terms on the Internet. Use the search terms "gender-neutral language."

Though we need to be sensitive to these issues of gender and age bias, writing that uses neutral language does not have to be dull. Using a positive and specific approach to convey a sharp meaning, while avoiding words and phrases that are age and gender biased, is achievable. We can learn how to write language that is engaging, specific, and alive. To convey an effective message, we will learn to use language that carefully considers word choice and its intended effect on its audience. Let us consider a few other topics that can help us keep our language crisp and engaging.

Clichés and Idioms
The differences between clichés and idioms are often not well understood. Clichés are overused expressions that have lost their meaning over time, i.e., "water under the bridge," whereas idioms are phrases that mean something other than the literal words in the phrase, i.e., "she's a thorn in my side" or "he's getting under my skin." Further, idioms have figurative rather than literal meanings, whereas clichés can be either figurative or literal. The Cambridge dictionary (Cambridge Dictionaries Online) describes an idiom as a group of words in a fixed order that have a particular meaning that is different from the meanings of each word understood on its own.

Because clichés and idioms tend to be overused in speech, in writing they should be avoided. Instead, use more specific descriptions of the idea or expression that you are trying to convey. At cliché.com you can find a very comprehensive list of clichés and their countries of origin. Check your own writing and avoid the use of these rather too familiar word choices (n.p., ClicheSite, Cliches, Euphemisms & Figures of Speech). Finally, if you do need to use an idiomatic expression to make a point in your writing, use the proper form of that expression.

Active vs. Passive Voice
Create engaging and dynamic language by using less passive voice and more energetic sentence formation. Beginning a sentence with phrases like "There is" or "It was determined" or "We were told by" are examples of passive construction.

Have you noticed the green lines that appear under many verbs in Microsoft Word when grammar checker is active? It will underline parts of the sentence in green if you are constructing a sentence in passive voice. Passive voice has this sentence construction: (noun) (verb phrase) by (noun). Why is this passive sentence construction not preferred? You want your main subject not relegated to the end of the sentence, following the word "by." Moreover, you want your subject to perform the action rather than to receive the action. As explained in the e-article "7 examples of Passive Voice," when the true subject is acted upon rather than acting, this weakens the sentence (Nichol, 2011).

Examples of Active vs. Passive Sentence Structure:

Passive:

> *"Forms and protocols shall be adhered to by the employees."*

Here the main subject or noun (employees) is relegated to the end of the sentence, making it a weak sentence structure, as we discussed previously.

Active:

> *"Employees shall adhere to these forms and protocols." OR*

> *"Employees will adhere to these forms and protocols." OR*

> *"Employees should adhere to these forms and protocols."*

In addition to using a stronger, less passive, sentence construction, where the main subject "employees" is now at the beginning of the sentence, this rewrite also uses fewer words to deliver the message.

Passive:

> *"The same principles should be applied to writing techniques for bulk MSM as for a single text message."*

Active:

> *"Apply the same writing techniques for bulk MSM as for a single text message."*

Microsoft Word contains both a spelling checking feature as well as a grammar checker. One of the most common sentence patterns that the grammar checker will flag with a green underline is the passive voice that we have been discussing. To see an explanation of the passive voice, simply click on the question mark in Word, above the toolbars to the right, and type "Passive Voice" in the Help Dialogue Box. The example shown below is easy to understand.

We have been discussing the importance of not overusing the passive voice. However, there are instances when you may want to use passive voice for various reasons. Sometimes, in fields such as politics, medicine, and law, to avoid being

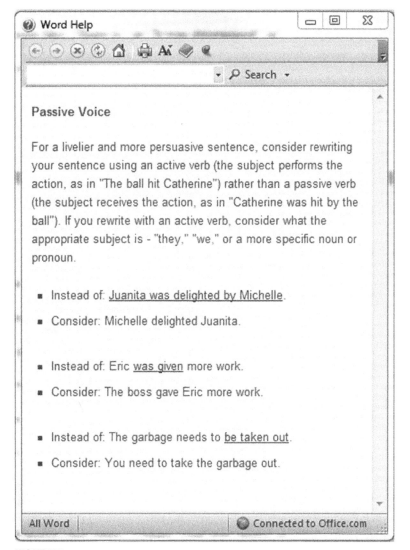

FIGURE 2

direct or assigning blame, a message will be softened by the use of passive voice. "Mistakes were made." "The patient was examined by me." "Cleansing of the area was performed." These are all examples of passive voice used not to assign primary responsibility and as established tones in a particular profession, where a primary actor does not need to be a part of the sentence. It is up to the writer to determine when passive voice is appropriate or conveys a stronger message.

■ **Mid-chapter Student Activity**

	Active	Passive
1.		
2.		
3.		
4.		
5.		

FIGURE 3

■ **Mid-chapter Student Activity**

	Clichés	Idioms
1.		
2.		
3.		
4.		
5.		

FIGURE 4

There are a few final considerations in relation to word choice before we move into sentence construction. Use acronyms with caution, and do not over use formal or technical language. Acronyms are words formed from other parts of words, such as "NATO" from the initial letters of the North Atlantic Treaty Organization. If you need to refer to an acronym repeatedly in a business document, then first write the words, followed by the acronym in parenthesis. Cascading Style Sheets (CSS), for example, should be written this way the first time it is used, but thereafter it can be referred to simply with the acronym CSS, without parentheses. If you are using acronyms within a particular business where the jargon is shared, then use the acronyms, again, sparingly, such as Cost Per Click (CPC) and Cost Per Action (CPA) in the marketing world. However, CPA, used in the accounting arena, stands for Certified Public Accountant, so use these terms in the proper setting and be certain that your audience understands this practice. The use of technical language shares similar concerns. Do not over use technical language, or use language that is so formal, so stilted, or so lofty that it is not understandable. Rather than impressing your audience with language that is overly formal, they will need more time to process language that is cumbersome and not used in a more familiar style.

■ Mid-chapter Student Activity

 Search for 20 acronyms related to marketing, sales, and the field of your interest to complete the Table Figure 5 below.

Acronym	Meaning

FIGURE 5

Sentence Design

Let us create a "best practices" checklist for effective sentence design:

BEST PRACTICES CHECKLIST FOR EFFECTIVE SENTENCE DESIGN	
What To Do	How To Achieve It
Organize the sentence.	Place nouns, verbs, and supporting clauses in the proper order.

Use supporting examples.	Make your assertion and follow with supporting examples.
Create emphasis.	Know your main or subordinate subject and place it properly in your sentence.
Avoid dangling and misplaced modifiers.	Keep the modifier with the noun it is referencing.
Avoid confusing word pairs.	Use words like "few and less" and "effect and affect" in the right context.
Use clarity in sentence design.	Economize on words. Write it or say it in a more concise and direct way. Write and revise to take out unnecessary, repetitive, or unclear words.
Create proper sentence length and vary it.	Vary the length of sentences in a paragraph to create reader interest.
Build sentence fluency.	Sentence length, transitions to the next sentence and language flow build sentence fluency.
Build parallelism in sentences.	Make words, phrases, and clauses match in their grammatical forms, including use of the same verb tense.
Use balance.	Use balanced independent clauses to create parallelism.

FIGURE 6

■ **Mid-chapter Student Activity**

Find examples for each of the "best practices" in Figure 6 above by Googling the term on the left hand side of the table.

Google this!	**I found this excellent example!** Copy and paste in the column below: 1. The URL (Web address of the site) 2. The supporting example
Organize the sentence.	

Use supporting examples.	
Create emphasis.	
Avoid dangling participles and prepositions at the end of the sentence.	
Avoid confusing words pairs.	
Use clarity in sentence design.	
Create proper sentence length and vary it.	
Build sentence fluency.	
Build parallelism.	
Use balance.	

FIGURE 7

Organize the Sentence Sentences should be logical and organized, and of proper length, to aid readers' understanding. Sentence organization drives comprehension. That was a short sentence, wasn't it? Sometimes a short sentence can be used for emphasis. However, in most cases, sentence structure will be longer to convey a more complex message. The magic of writing is to create order and interest and to strike a balance between a sentence that is too short and that may seem abrupt, or too long, which may bore the reader. Readability studies show that the longer the sentence, the more difficult it is for the reader to understand.

We want to convey order to the reader or listener. To do this, we use patterns. For example, a simple sentence must have a few common parts: an article, a subject, and a verb. The most common articles in the English language are "the," "a," or, "an," and "some." Examine this simple sentence.

Article	Subject	Verb
A	company	thrives.

FIGURE 8

This sentence is grammatically correct, but it does not convey as much data as a curious reader would want to know. So we use words that soften or introduce the subject or verb to give them more specific and subtle meaning. Articles, for example, suggest in the listener's mind whether the thought or idea is many or few (singular or plural), masculine, or feminine. Prepositions such as "on," "beneath," "against," and "beside" are linking words that connect nouns, pronouns, and phrases to other words in the sentence. In this case, usually the relationship is temporal, spatial, or logical. Adjectives modify a noun and adverbs modify or further define or describe an action. Additional linking words, such as adjectives, adverbs, and phrases, convey ideas that are even more complex, thus making the writing more specific, complete, and interesting.

Our minds want to draw logical conclusions. One way we do this is by using patterns in writing. Grammar is a patterned way of expressing logic. The patterns that we use in writing should be consistent and well balanced, like pairing yellow with yellow and blue with blue. They provide the reader with more information, from which they can formulate a response.

Now consider the simple sentence we formulated before, but with a few more grammatical elements: the adjective, the adverb, and a prepositional phrase.

Article	Adjective	Noun	Adverb	Verb	Prepositional Phrase
A	new	company	undoubtedly	thrives	on creative energy.

FIGURE 9

As we add more modifiers and phrases to the above sentence, you can see how the complexity of the idea or expressions builds.

At an adult writing level, we do not have to think of sentences in such simple terms. We simply write or speak, given the level of reading and the spoken language that we have acquired. We then return to the writing and examine it. At this point we check for organization in the sentence, make sure we have followed good writing principles, reconstruct the sentence in the editing process to avoid negative writing structures, and determine if it feels like interesting writing.

Article	Adjective	Noun	Adverb	Verb	Prepositional Phrase	Supporting Example
A	new	company	undoubtedly	thrives	on creative energy,	as the Advertising Department's inventive and successful "T-shirt Campaign" demonstrates.

FIGURE 10

Use Supporting Examples   In this illustration, we add a supporting example at the end of the sentence, replacing the period with a comma to extend the thought and the sentence.

The use of supporting examples in sentences cannot be overrated. It is the evidence that supports the assertion you make at the beginning of the sentence. It creates even more concrete understanding in the reader. The canvas develops and the reader gets a better picture of what you are expressing as more information unfolds in its proper place. Employers often give feedback regarding the applications of job candidates who assert that they have specific skills, but who fail to list their skills in response to those stated. If a candidate states, "I have led extensive successful marketing campaigns," then details of at least one of those campaigns should be the next sentence in the e-mail response and the resume. Making an unsupported assertion, or an idea without enough supporting ideas to reinforce or validate the assertion, creates bewilderment and doubt in the reader.

Create Emphasis   Giving ideas priority in a sentence or in related sentences involves determining what is primary and secondary, then where the main ideas should be placed. There are two primary ways to manage emphasis.

1. Subordinate clause

   For this structure, place main ideas in the first part of the sentence, and secondary or subsequent clauses behind them. Consider the main idea and subordinate clause below.

   "A new company undoubtedly thrives on creative energy, *as* the Advertising Department's inventive and successful "T-shirt Campaign" demonstrates."

2. Equal Emphasis

To give equal emphasis, create balanced ideas on each side of the equation, often in separate main clauses separated by the word "and." Consider the addition of the word "and" to give equal emphasis to both main clauses.

"A new company undoubtedly thrives on creative energy, *and* the Advertising Department's inventive and successful "T-shirt Campaign" demonstrates this."

Avoid Dangling Modifiers

What is a dangling modifier? In sentence construction, if there is an action verb in any part of your sentence it must be matched with a living thing or machine that performs the action. Rearranging the sentence takes care of misplaced modifiers, but not dangling modifiers. To fix a dangling modifier construction, you must add a word or words to the sentence.

Two excellent examples of dangling modifiers are cited below from the free Internet site (n.p., Participles & Misplaced Modifiers atpppst.com).

▩ Examples of Dangling Modifiers

The excitement was palpable, staring out over the audience.

- ▩ *Explanation:* The <u>excitement</u> is not alive, and it is not a machine. It cannot stare anywhere. Add a person.

- ■ "Staring out over the audience, Johnny saw that the excitement was palpable."

- ■ "When in grade school, my mother went back to college."

  - ▩ *Explanation:* This is a matter of logic—my mother could not have gone back to college in 3rd grade.

- ■ "When I was in grade school, my mother went back to college."

Avoid Misplaced Modifiers

A misplaced modifier is a modifier that is incorrectly separated from the word or words it describes. This leads to misunderstanding by the reader or listener. Place the modifier as close as possible to words it describes.

▩ Misplaced modifier:

- ■ "Kathryn *almost* coughed throughout the entire PowerPoint presentation."

▩ Corrected version:

- ■ "Kathryn coughed almost throughout the entire PowerPoint presentation."

Avoid Confusing Words Pairs There are noteworthy confusing word pairs, or words that are close in spelling but have different meanings. If you have doubt about your use of these confusing terms, simply look them up in a dictionary built into your word processor, or online. Some that may be found in business writing include the following.

■ Mid-chapter Student Activity

Find the definition of each word in Figure 11 using a dictionary resource, then find five more of your own confusing word pairs to add to the list.

CONFUSING WORD PAIRS	
Affect	Effect
Accept	Except
Their	They're
Lie	Lay
Sit	Set

FIGURE 11

Using Clarity To Build Concise and Clear Sentences Writing effectively involves using language that is clear and concise. Therefore, one of the most important techniques to use in building sentences is to eliminate extra words. Another way to say this is that we want to economize on words. When I ask students to send me an electronic copy of their resume during the job search portion of my class, I tell them "more is better" because I cannot create or fictionalize their real life jobs. Then I immediately follow that with the expectation that much of what the student adds, I will remove or restructure. This technique is economizing with language. It is a process that can only occur when there is more than one review of the business message or report. We remember that writing is a process that takes time, and that when we put our thoughts on paper, it takes many iterations to organize them to assure that the intended effect occurs. Business professionals and business writing students have acquired a level of writing proficiency that, in most cases, allows them to see their own excess use of words—simply by taking the time to reexamine the document. Just take some time away from the written piece, then look at it again and ask, "How can I say the same thing with fewer words?" We will be practicing this technique is Chapter Five as we draft our business documents.

Sentence Length

What is appropriate sentence length? The response to this question relates to readability studies and formulas conducted over the past 80 years. Some landmark studies have survived application, investigation, and more than a bit of controversy over this period of time. Much research has been published on the topic of readability. According to Dubay (2004), George Klare (1963) defines readability as "the ease of understanding or comprehension due to the style of writing." Similarly, Hargis and her colleagues' findings at IBM (1998) show that readability is the "ease of reading words and sentences" and an aspect of clarity. Interaction of the reader and the text is shown in the SMOG readability study, adding to the formerly established factor of comprehensibility, the element of the subject matter being compelling to the reader. Finally, the most comprehensive definition may be that of Edgar Dale and Jeanne Chall (1949), which includes the sum total of all elements within the material and the success that readers have with it.

A very obvious and compelling example related to car seat installation instructions illustrates the importance of audience readability. DuBay cites a study by Dr. Mark Wegner and Deborah Girasek (2003) who referred to adult literacy studies that led them to conclude that of the 107 instructions they examined on the car seats they were studying, they found the writing to be at the 10th grade level, too difficult for 80% of readers to comprehend. Studies showed that 79 to 94 percent of car seats are used improperly. Another study by Kahane (1986) showed that fatal injury is reduced by 71 percent and hospitalization by 67 percent when child safety seats are properly installed. Wegner and Girasek suspected that poor comprehension of the instructions may have contributed significantly to this car seat installation problem.

More readability research ensued. DuBay goes on to cite that by the 1980s over 200 readability formulas were developed. These readability formulas use factors such as ASL, Average Sentence Length, and ASW, Average Word Length in Syllables.

ASL = Average Sentence Length

W = Number of Words in the text

S = Number of Words in the sentence

ASL = W divided by S, or W ÷ S

Therefore, to calculate the average sentence lengths in your own writing, count the total number of words in the paragraph or passage and divide by the number of sentences in the text.

So how do these readability studies help you as a writer? Readability formulas help writers in relation to preferred and effective level of words and sentences. It helps you analyze your writing, keep within average sentence lengths so the reader understands your writing, and write to the level of your audience. The very popular Flesch-Kincaid Grade-Level Formula "correlates 0.91 with comprehension as measured by reading tests" (http://en.wikipedia.org) and is found in popular word processing software such as Microsoft Word. They help us direct the level of our writing to our audience. Interestingly, over time, sentences have become shorter, as noted by Sherman (1893), by comparing works from Pre-Elizabethan times at 50 words per sentence, to Sherman's time at about 29 words per sentence, to the current average of 20 words per sentence, as evidenced by various writing manuals.

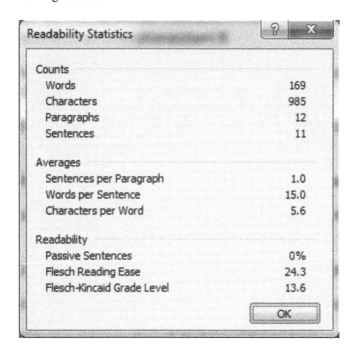

FIGURE 12 *Readability Statistics.*

In summary, the most appropriate average English sentence length for most pieces of writing is 15 to 20 words. However, some academic writing may have 30 words or more in a sentence. Nevertheless, for business writing, the common

15 to 20 words per sentence recommendation is a wise practice. In subsequent chapters, we will see that some sentences are crafted shorter intentionally to create impact.

Once the level of the writer and the sum total of the elements that affect the readers' success in understanding the material are taken into consideration, other factors such as organization, coherence, transitions, and tone affect our success in writing.

Sentence Fluency The length of a sentence is just one factor involved in creating sentences that flow. Other factors involved in sentence fluency include the rhythm and flow of the sentence, varying the length of sentences appropriately in a paragraph, and making proper transitions from one sentence to another and from one paragraph to another. Paying attention to the sound of the words used is important as well, because readers and listeners like language that is pleasing to the ear.

Have you met a friend or a colleague who had what seemed like a "natural" ability to write or to speak? A person that seemed to write or speak effortlessly and whose audience read or sat in rapture of that writing or speech? Some individuals do seem to master these skills more readily than others do; however, it is very important to know and believe that good writing and good speaking can be learned, and mastered. In this text, you are striving to achieve a level of mastery with your own writing. Let us intentionally use a cliché here: "Practice makes perfect!" To say that practice will make "perfect" writing is unrealistic, as we are attempting to create effective language, and language can be effectively written in a number of different styles. Nevertheless, the message is that through practice, one becomes a better writer.

Creating the Excellent Paragraph

Once we have mastered the art of creating engaging and concise sentences, we need to join the sentences together to form excellent paragraphs. Excellent paragraphs contain excellent sentences as well as effective transitions between the sentences. Paragraphs have, at the very least, three essential components: 1) the topic or introductory sentence, 2) supporting sentences, and 3) a concluding or summary sentence.

The topic sentence is critically important in directing the reader, as it introduces the main idea of the paragraph. After writing the topic sentence, follow the assertion or introduction with supporting sentences containing facts and examples. Make sure that, as you develop the paragraph, these supporting sentences continue to relate to the introductory sentence. Finally, the concluding sentence or sentences not only summarize the paragraph, but also should contain a transitional sentence leading to the next paragraph.

We can develop this argument further, anticipating that the paragraphs need to be joined to form a related document with a sound beginning, content in the middle paragraphs and a concluding paragraph that nicely summarizes the information. Not all documents will be lengthy, especially business documents that seem to fly back and forth with lightning speed given the predominant use of e-mail and the Internet. But the organized use of an opening or introductory sentence, followed by sentences and paragraphs with supporting examples, and a conclusion is a pattern that can be adapted to documents of varying lengths.

This site, (http://www.grammar.cccc.commnet.edu/grammar), contains extensive online grammar lessons, examples, and quizzes, developed by English faculty written at a Midwestern university, as well as by students in Professor Karyn Hollis's Tutor Training course at Villanova University. It is made available online by Evelyn Farbman and the publisher, Houghton Mifflin Inc.

A good final test of your writing is to ask the "who," "what," "where," "when," "how," and "why" of a sentence that you craft. You do not have to answer each of these questions in every sentence that you write, but at the end of the paragraph, after you have linked related sentences together, you should check the message to make sure you have included most of these questions.

Building Paragraphs That Flow with Transitions Another final consideration in writing is to create paragraphs that flow. Unify them in thought and have a clear beginning, middle, and end. Good paragraphs use transitional words and phrases to make the connections between sentences and paragraphs smooth and understandable for the reader. Beautiful and effective writing walks the reader through ideas effortlessly, with proper connections. Providing these transitions is a matter of being conscious of the fact that your reader does not know what you are trying to express.

To achieve these connections, use little conjunctions such as "and," "but," "nor," "for," "yet," or, "so." Transitional expressions include words like "however," "moreover," "nevertheless," and "on the other hand." Another technique that makes reading easier to understand is to repeat key words or phrases. Be creative and use various conjunctive words and expressions rather than overusing the same connectors.

Building Parallelism and Balance Balance and parallelism are very important final considerations that make your writing feel consistent and smooth. Parallel construction uses likeness of form in expressions that have similar content and function. Thus, the reader recognizes more easily likeness of content and function (http://grammar.ccc.commnet.edu/

grammar/parallelism.htm).

A beautiful example of parallel writing is exemplified in Abraham Lincoln's "Gettysburg Address" delivered at Gettysburg on November 19, 1863.

**Abraham Lincoln's
Gettysburg Address**

Delivered at Gettysburg on November 19, 1863

Fourscore and seven years ago our fathers brought forth on this continent a new nation, conceived in liberty and dedicated to the proposition that all men are created equal.

Now we are engaged in a great civil war, testing whether that nation or any nation so conceived and so dedicated can long endure. We are met on a great battle field of that war. We have come to dedicate a portion of that field, as a final resting place for those who here gave their lives that that nation might live. It is altogether fitting and proper that we should do this.

But, in a larger sense, we can not dedicate—we can not consecrate—we can not hallow—this ground. The brave men, living and dead, who struggled here, have consecrated it, far above our poor power to add or detract. The world will little note, nor long remember, what we say here, but it can never forget what they did here. It is for us the living, rather, to be dedicated here to the unfinished work which they who fought here have thus far so nobly advanced. It is rather for us to be here dedicated to the great task remaining before us—that from these honored dead we take increased devotion to that cause for which they gave the last full measure of devotion—that we here highly resolve that these dead shall not have died in vain—that this nation, under God, shall have a new birth of freedom—and that government of the people, by the people, for the people, shall not perish from the earth.

Click on the movie icon for a brief "slide-show" that will illustrate some of (but not all) of the various patterns of parallelism within the Gettysburg Address. First, though, you might want to print out this copy and connect the various phrases in parallel form yourself. The exercise will take about a minute and a half to complete, depending on your connection and your browser.

Sorry, no time right now. Take me back!

http://grammar.ccc.commnet.edu/grammar/gettysburg/gettysburg16.html

Fourscore and seven years ago our fathers brought forth on this continent a new nation, conceived in liberty and dedicated to the proposition that all men are created equal.

Now we are engaged in a great civil war, testing whether that nation or any nation so conceived and so dedicated can long endure. We are met on a great battle field of that war. We have come to dedicate a portion of that field as a final resting place for those who here gave their lives that that nation might live. It is altogether fitting and proper that we should do this.

But, in a larger sense, we can not dedicate—we can not consecrate—we can not hallow—this ground. The brave men, living and dead, who struggled here, have consecrated it, far above our poor power to add or detract. The world will little note, nor long remember, what we say here, but it can never forget what they did here. It is for us the living, rather, to be dedicated here to the unfinished work which they who fought here have thus far so nobly advanced. It is rather for us to be here dedicated to the great task remaining before us—that from these honored dead we take increased devotion to that cause for which they gave the last full measure of devotion—that we here highly resolve that these dead shall not have died in vain—that this nation, under God, shall have a new birth of freedom—and that government of the people, by the people, for the people shall not perish from the earth.

FIGURE 13 ca-webmaster@ccc.commnet.edu

Paragraph Length What is an appropriate and effective paragraph length? We consider this in relation to sentence length as well. Generally, we want paragraphs to be unified in thought. We want to introduce the idea, support the idea, then conclude the idea. We want to do this in as concise a space as possible, without compromising content and style. Also, as we vary sentence length, we want to vary paragraph length.

Whole Document Considerations

The final step in the writing process involves looking at your document as a complete communication, with a beginning, middle, and an end. The paragraphs should flow smoothly, use the right types of transitional words and expressions, and build the logic of the message in an organized fashion. Read and revise liberally. Take out unneeded words with each revision. Check the tone to assure that the communication has the proper degree of formality; in all cases, the tone should be positive, even if the message may contain some negative news or facts.

Final Formatting Considerations

First, use the spelling and grammar checker! In Word, spelling errors are underlined in red and grammar errors are underlined in green. Refer to the built in reviewing tools. They include Spelling & Grammar, Research, Thesaurus, Word Count, and Translations. Also, there are unlimited resources on the Internet, such as manuals of style, grammar assistance Websites with extensive explanations, examples, and quizzes, many of them free and published by colleges and universities. Make use of the templates feature in the File Menu in Word. There are hundreds of samples of business documents, as well as research and academic documents. Compare your work against these professionally crafted documents, checking formatting and content.

The Response

If the message was effectively crafted and delivered, the chances of the initial communicator getting a positive response are higher. The final step for the recipient is to respond to the message, making the recipient the new initiating communicator. The writing cycle begins all over again!

Feedback: A New Step in the 3-Step Writing Process. Revision, Changing Behavior and Follow-up

Feedback is a very important part of making any communication work. It is a process whereby after you have determined which type of communication to send, you then adjust your style and content to the response from your intended recipient(s). This adjustment is very important to your growth in the company and to your success with your end goal, whether it is to increase profits and decrease cost, to streamline operations, to reach a broader base of customers, or to lead to more satisfied employees or customers.

As we discussed in Chapter One, feedback is a key component of creating positive ongoing communication that changes as the context changes and dictates.

At this point, you may consider discussing the response with a colleague, reviewing it again, then editing and sending a response (to the response). This back and forth communication process can occur over an extended time. Much of it occurs via e-mail in today's Internet connected business world.

A practical consideration is to maintain a consistent "**Subject**" line in your e-mail. That way, you can search for the communication string and retrieve all messages related to that particular common subject string.

FIGURE 14

This is an excellent way to see the history of the communications, to ensure that the next response in the chain has appropriate content and tone, and that it goes to the appropriate people as well.

Finally, with today's technology, it is easy to send documents quickly. However, crafting the idea into an effective piece of writing takes many iterations to come to final form. One of the most common errors made in sending written communications is not anticipating the number of revisions that are required to bring the document to an effective and concise form. To control this tendency, it is important to allow time to revise a document an appropriate number of times before sending.

Positive News, Neutral News, Bad News Messages, Persuasive Messages, and Reports

Chapter Four

Learning Objectives

LO1 Compose a routine inquiry and a positive response to a Routine Inquiry

LO2 Write a negative response to a Routine Inquiry

LO3 Deliver Good News

LO4 Compose a Bad News Response

LO5 Compose a message that builds Good Will

LO6 Identify The AIDA Approach

LO7 Compose a Persuasive Response to a Denied Claim

LO8 Identify the Problem/Solution Approach in an appeal

LO9 Describe the elements of an Effective Sales Campaign

LO10 Describe the importance of Social Media, Online Advertising, and E-mail Marketing Campaigns

LO11 Compose and present a Persuasive Request, a White Paper, and a Power-Point presentation

LO12 Post a Persuasive Request, a White Paper, and a PowerPoint presentation to your student blog site as instructed.

Apply all of the excellent writing techniques discussed and illustrated in the preceding chapters in your Positive News, Neutral News, and Negative News messages. Keep the tone positive throughout the message and end with good will to ensure ongoing positive business relationships. Additionally, for all messages, structure the paragraphs and arrange the questions logically. In a response, arrange the answers to the questions in the order in which they appear.

The Routine Inquiry

Many messages sent via e-mail are routine "business as usual" inquiries or letters. You are either asking for routine information or you are giving routine information. These letters are often referred to as routine inquiry or request letters. The sender is requesting information from the recipient or sending information to the recipient. Routine inquiries can be inter-organizational, going to colleagues or peers inside the organization, or external, going to clients or vendors outside the organization. The routine request letter should contain approximately four paragraphs.

The opening paragraph is most effective when it is direct. In other words, be specific about the information that you are requesting or delivering. The content paragraph or paragraphs further explain or request precise or detailed information. The closing paragraph should extend goodwill and ask for action.

- Opening paragraph—use a direct approach,

- Content Paragraph—specific questions, often broken down into bullets or numbered items and multiple paragraphs with more information and clarity or requesting more data,

- Closing paragraph(s)—should extend good will and ask for action.

The letter should include the following information:

TO: Jackie Martin, Owner

FROM: Student Name (Your Name)

SUBJECT: Business Writing with an Edge Business Model

You will be asking for a meeting. During that meeting, you want to ask permission to peruse the Business Plan for "Business Writing With An Edge" because you consider it a successful business model. You go on to explain that you are interested in creating your own online company, and that blogs will be included in that company. You want to know the statistics related to our blogs, such as the number of hits and the profile of the audience accessing the site. You want to share this with your potential business partners for a presentation for investors in your online business. Use current dates and be as specific as possible. You may add your own details and questions. Include a closing paragraph that creates goodwill and asks for a meeting within a week. Use your name for the signature.

■ **Mid-chapter Student Activity, 1(a)**

 Using Word, search for "Business Letter Templates" using the "File" "New" menu choices. "File" "New" in any version of Microsoft Word will take you to both built-in local templates and online templates that are updated frequently. Choose a routine inquiry template (search for it) and use it to create your own Routine Inquiry Letter.

The Response to a Routine Inquiry

In the previous examples, you sent a routine inquiry letter. If the anticipatory set is positive between you and an established business partner, then write a direct response. The direct response answers the questions posed, in a logical order. Alternatively, if the inquiry provided more information to either assist with the inquiry or to add to a previous correspondence, then acknowledge it and thank your sender.

Positive Response to a Routine Inquiry The primary objective in a favorable response to a routine inquiry is to tell your reader what the person wants to know. Therefore, a direct response begins with the answer to the question(s). If there is just one question, then answer that. If

[Your Name]
[Street Address]
[City, ST ZIP Code]
July 25, 2012

[Recipient Name]
[Title]
[Company Name]
[Street Address]
[City, ST ZIP Code]

Dear: [Recipient Name]:

This is a reminder that we still need some information from you in order to include your entry in the Word Press Blog "Business Writing With An Edge." for next month's March entry. There are two considerations for the entry:

1. Design and Layout – we will be including only those entries that use the "Business Writing With An Edge" logo (jpeg logo attached).

2. Permissions and Disclaimer Pages – we will need your signature on both these pages (attached) and for you to return them in PDF format.

Documents need to be received by February 28. Please note that this is an absolute deadline. If we do not have the material in our hands by 5 P.M., the three pages devoted to your products will be taken out of the catalog.

If there is anything we can do to assist you, please let me know.

Sincerely,

[Your Name]
[Title]

FIGURE 1 *Example, Routine Inquiry Letter.*

there are more, than you may want to bullet or enumerate the list using the built-in features in Word in or a similar word processing program.

■ Mid-chapter Student Activity, 1(b)

Using the Business Writing with an Edge Business Model Memo from Student Activity 1(a), write a Positive Response to your Routine Inquiry. It should be

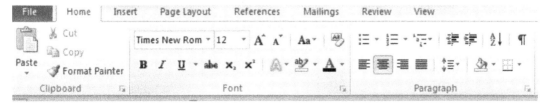

FIGURE 2

a three-paragraph response, with an Opening and Content and Closing Paragraphs. Use the direct writing approach.

The Refused Request—A Negative Response to a Routine Inquiry

In this scenario, your reader has asked for something—a meeting and your business plan—but you must say no. There will be times when the recipient is unable to fulfill a proposed request. Sometimes even trusted business associates and colleagues ask us for information that we just cannot, or should not, provide as it may result in a compromise of values, or data, or shared resources. It is extremely important in these cases that the tone remain positive when delivering the bad news and that you still express goodwill. So let us consider this alternative response. If it is necessary that the inquiry be met with some degree of negative response, how do we present the information?

In this case then, should we still use the direct approach, answering the question first? We can employ another tactic. Because we want to minimize the impact of negative news, we want to use an indirect approach, reordering the information, so that we are reinforcing the good relationship that we have, and preparing the reader for some additional information or implications that the person may not have considered previously. After some negotiating, this further exchange may result in benefits for the reader in the end.

In your student activity, 1(a) you have written a request to a business associate, at Business Writing With An Edge, asking for a meeting during which she might share her business model with you. You are expecting a favorable response, but are surprised. The response is not favorable, in fact, it needs to delicately deliver a bad news message.

So wear the opposite business hat. You are the recipient of that request; in fact, you are the president of the company "Business Writing With An Edge" and you are actually surprised at reading the request for you to share your business model with her. You invented the company. It was your brainchild, and you have put much time and energy into building it to its current successful position. You need to think about this response.

In this next scenario, you will need to soften the news. You still want to include the three to four paragraphs that we included in the "positive response to a routine inquiry":

1. Opening Paragraph,
2. Content Paragraph, and
3. Closing Paragraph.

but note that the descriptors are different.

1. Opening paragraph—use an indirect approach,
2. Content Paragraph—specific explanations as to why the request cannot be fulfilled, often broken down into bullets or numbered items and multiple paragraphs with more information and clarity,
3. Closing paragraph(s)—should extend good will and ask for understanding, not action, and offer an alternative solution, if possible.

■ **Mid-chapter Student Activity, 1(c)**

 Write a negative response to the routine inquiry asking for a meeting time to discuss the business plan of Business Writing With An Edge. Keep the above guidelines in mind, as you are now writing an indirect response to soften the message. Use transitional phrases such as "Though we value your friendship" for the opening paragraph or "In continued collaboration" for the closing paragraph and "It violates our privacy rules" or "all stakeholders may not agree" for the content paragraphs. You are encouraged to add your own indirect and softening language as well. Remember, this is a relationship you want to keep!

Adjustment Grants—Delivering Good News in Response to a Claim

The adjustment grant message, written in response to a complaint that results in the company making an error, is a good news message. A customer is dissatisfied with some level of service that your company or organization has provided, and is asking for you to rectify that. Because the client is the person you serve and without that person you would not have a business, it is always important to place the client's concerns first.

In this first scenario, we will be able to write an adjustment letter in a very positive fashion, as the error was actually in house. If it is your company that has made the error, then you will want to extend your service beyond normal levels to maintain good will, and, most importantly, so that the customer will return. Even if your service is something that a person will only consume once, such as a home purchase if you are a mortgage broker, for example, you will want to be aware of the information or image that customer will provide externally to the general public. This public relations network and image that builds among consumers is critical to building and maintaining a client base.

Therefore, this response begins with a direct approach, identifying the transaction immediately, with detail, and using a positive tone. Provide more details if necessary in the middle or content paragraphs. Include part numbers, dollar amounts, dates, locations. This is where the "who," "what," "when," "where," and "how" principle applies. Close, thanking the customer for his loyalty and stating that you look forward to his continued business.

Adjustment Grants—Delivering Bad News in Response to a Claim That Is Denied

A request for an adjustment letter that is denied is a bit more difficult to compose. In this case, a customer is requesting something that the company is unwilling to provide. It may be outside of the realm of company policy or procedure or it may be due to the consumer's action or position. When the consumer is at fault to such a degree that the company needs to let the client know that the request is unreasonable and cannot ultimately be fulfilled, the message has to be softened and carefully crafted. The company has to take the chance of even losing that customer's business.

Imagine this possible consumer-business dynamic. A consumer is approaching a car dealership for a $3,000 engine repair bill when her car's 100,000-mile warranty is 10,000 miles out of the warranty period. Perhaps this consumer takes the approach of trying to convince the dealership that because she has been a loyal customer for 20 years, the dealership should honor the warranty anyhow. Clearly, a company would have to write the message carefully, as a rather unreasonable recipient will receive it.

In this case, begin by thanking the client for her loyalty, let her know that you understand her request, then move gently to the "however" or "though" stage of the communication, letting her know that her request cannot be fulfilled.

Then support your statement with examples in your content paragraphs. In the example of the car dealership, company policy, a reminder that the warranty has been out of date for 10,000 miles, and any other pertinent data can be presented in bulleted fashion. Close with a very strong affirmation once again, that you appreciate her business, and that you will continue to value her as a loyal client—in spite of the negative response that you may expect to receive back from her!

TO: Client First Name, Client Last Name

FROM: Company Representative Name, Title

SUBJECT: Claim Number 123

"We appreciate your loyalty to XYZ Automotive." We also understand the intent of your communication. Though we appreciate you as a customer and have every intent to continue to service your account to the best of our ability, the request that you are making to extend the warranty is not within our company's ability to fulfill."

- ▓ The warranty that we have on file for your account, number 1234, expired at 100,000 miles. Your odometer reads 101,000 miles.

- ▓ Our company policy states on page xx, that warranties cannot be honored after the mileage limit has been reached.

We do of course look forward to providing you with excellent service at XYZ Automotive. If you have any further questions regarding this claim, please contact: Company Representative Name, Title

---

FIGURE 3 *Example, Adjustment Grants Delivering Bad News, in Response to a Claim that is Denied*

Note that in the final paragraph it is not necessary or wise to call attention back to the problem, or to apologize. Simply accentuate the positive communication and the hope for continued good relations.

Messages That Build Good Will

Online Orders and Acknowledgements Routine inquiries in today's online business environment are often managed by databases. The database automatically sends a confirmation of the request with all pertinent details and contact information. These messages are extremely important to build and keep a strong client database in any business or organization. In our technology savvy world, these routine tasks are often handled with software, not by a customer service representative.

For example, airline, hotel, and car reservations, event reservations, ordering from online stores, and information gathering are processes that are not handled by customer service representatives, but rather by an online form-filling process.

The common denominator in all online business transactions, the piece that allows the company or organization to communicate directly with the consumer, is the e-mail address.

The online application process involves:

- Knowing the Website or URL of the company

- Visiting that site and filling out their form, with dates, times, item number, and any other related data

- Providing your e-mail address and filling out a credit card page, if it is a monetary transaction

- Hitting the "Submit" button or something similar to send the data to their company server

- Receiving an order acknowledgement with a confirmation and/or history of that transaction in your e-mail inbox

Some requests may become complicated. Travel tickets may not arrive on time, seats may need to be reassigned at an event, or the consumer may need to cancel or reschedule a reservation. In all of these cases, it is important to have the history of the transaction, then call or write to the customer service representative that can assist you with your issue.

One-on-one communication is difficult to find in organizations today. There are many layers of communication, and customer service workers with only certain privileges to handle certain pieces of business, are placed intentionally at the front end of customer service, to protect those in management. Those who have the authority to make decisions regarding the handling of the customer's more difficult situation are very difficult to reach by phone. It can most certainly be a frustrating situation for the customer, as personal attention from someone who can make higher level decisions and move the transaction along more quickly seems to become harder and harder to negotiate.

Good Will Messages of Praise or Congratulations

Sending praise or congratulations messages for a job well done is an often overlooked form of communication. This form of message has intrinsic value as people need to know that they are recognized, needed, and valued in an organization, as well as in their lives in general. Taking a few moments to compose an e-mail message to a colleague for a presentation that was delivered well, or for a meeting that went well, or for some other success that the person has achieved in life, builds trust and camaraderie and makes the person feel like a valued and visible member of the team. This type of good will communication goes a long way in building, maintaining, and preserving relationships.

Summary

Some important points to remember in good news, neutral news, and bad news messages:

- If the message is favorable,

  - then a direct response is appropriate.

- If the message is negative,

  - then use the indirect approach.

  - Emphasize the good news and subordinate the bad news.

- Timing is a very important consideration.

  - Deliver the news when it will be best received.

- Collect data pertinent to the claim or request.

  - Facts must be accurate to ensure the validity of your position.

- Use a positive tone, even when the news is negative.

  - This creates the best chance of continued good will in the relationship.

- Use simple tables, bullets, and numbered items to organize your data.

  - These are automatic functions built into Word.

Persuasive Messages

In previous chapters, we have spoken at great length about creating good will. We also addressed the importance of knowing your audience and having a "you-centered" approach. When writing persuasive messages, it is even more important to keep these two important practices in mind. If your request is not a simple direct request, where you are anticipating a positive outcome, but complicated and uncertain regarding how the recipient will respond to your request, then a persuasive appeal is in order. Knowing something about the reader and his anticipatory set will help you adjust the message to him. Making even more of an effort to maintain good positive language, while trying to persuade is equally critical.

We are all familiar with persuasive messages, such as sales pitches, TV commercials, flyers, brochures, and online ads that bombard us daily, but they do not all get our attention to the same degree or at the same time. Some may not get our attention at all. We want to focus in this chapter on persuasive messages that achieve the intended goal and reach the intended market audience.

The AIDA Approach

Given that the persuasive message is not a simple, direct routine message, it is necessary to strategize regarding the message, the target, and the delivery. Persuasive messages must call the attention of the reader. Once calling attention, they must engage the reader. To be engaged, it must be interesting to the reader. Next, the message must convince the reader to follow the course of action that you are persuading him or her to follow, and finally it must make it easy for the reader to follow up on that course of action. We can look back in time a bit at the history of some of advertising's experts who developed these principles and the AIDA system.

First the principles!
The AIDA approach to advertising is commonly attributed to E. St. Elmo Lewis. He attributed the following three principles to which advertising should conform:

> *The mission of an advertisement is to attract a reader, so that he will look at the advertisement and start to read it; then to interest him, so that he will continue to read it; then to convince him, so that when he has read it he will believe it.* (Lewis)

The general concept was also mentioned by several other advertising experts around the mid 1800s to the early 1900s. The first published concept occurred in 1904, in an article by Frank Hutchinson Dukesmith; but the first instance of the acronym itself was in an article by C. P. Russell in 1921, where he wrote:

> *An easy way to remember this formula is to call in the "law of association," which is the old reliable among memory aids. It is to be noted that, reading downward, the first letters of these words spell the opera "Aida." When you start a letter, then, say "Aida" to yourself and you won't go far wrong, at least as far as the form of your letter is concerned.* (Russell, 1921)

Then the practice!

- **Attention (Awareness):** attract the attention of the customer.

- **I—Interest:** raise customer interest by focusing on and demonstrating advantages and benefits (instead of focusing on features, as in traditional advertising).

▪ **D—Desire:** convince customers that they want and desire the product or service and that it will satisfy their needs.

▪ **A—Action:** lead customers towards taking action and/or purchasing.

So, in persuasive messages, we will incorporate these principles and practices. Examine the practices before writing the message, strategize for each point, and, when the message is finished, check your writing against the AIDA checklist as well.

Persuasive Requests

A persuasive message is an indirect message. You do not want to simply state in direct terms right away that you want your requests met. You must build up to the argument and persuade with examples, keeping a positive tone. A strategy needs to be employed to persuade the reader to agree with you. There are two primary choices often used in the opening. 1) You can set up the explanation for the reader to choose what you are suggesting, or 2) you can state the problem and the solution in more overarching terms.

Setting Up the Explanation In the first situation, let us return to the example of the Denied Request that was sent to the client by XYZ Automotive. The client has now received that denial letter and is writing a persuasive letter back. After all, $3,000 is a lot of money!

The client uses the "setting up the explanation" approach. Using a soft approach, the letter opening may read something like this:

"Dear XYZ Automotive. Thank you for your response dated xxx. I understand why according to company policy you would not be able to immediately make a decision to reimburse me for the $3,000 request for engine repairs. I believe I may have erred in not providing enough information for you to make that decision."

FIGURE 4 *Opening paragraph.*

Do you see how the writer is using the indirect approach, not making any demands immediately, but rather easing into the situation? The writer is even admitting that she could have provided more information to you—an excellent way of providing an "explanation opening." Let's move on to the Content Paragraphs.

The Content Paragraphs then provide more information and further explanation.

"I failed to report that my car was in your shop for repair two years previous to the date of the engine repair. At that time, the odometer was supposedly fixed. As it turns out, I took it to another shop and they repaired it properly and told me that it actually had been set to 'overstate' the mileage by 1,200 miles.

"This means that actually my car was still under warranty when the engine repair was performed at your shop on xxx date. I have attached a PDF file as evidence of the dates and repairs."

FIGURE 5 *Content paragraphs.*

What a reaction this will provoke in the reader at XYZ Automotive! This changes the entire dynamic of the transaction and the appropriate response. Clearly, there will need to be further investigation into the matter. Then the writer needs to move on to a closing that will reinstate good will, and ask in a firmer fashion for action and follow up.

"Thank you for taking the time to carefully consider this new information. I would like to request a phone call within the next five working days. I can best be reached at 123-456-7890."

FIGURE 6 *Closing.*

Note that the closing paragraph has a very gracious tone in the first line, but the last line shows a firm tone about requesting action. In Figure 5.7, we see the entire message put together.

■ **Mid-chapter Student Activity, 2**

 Answer the following questions in Word in a one page document, double spaced.

Questions to ask:

1. Did the opener get the attention of the reader?
2. Was the approach used an indirect approach?
3. Does the explanation set up the course of action or further discussion?

TO: Client First Name, Client Last Name

FROM: Company Representative Name, Title

SUBJECT: Claim Number 123

Dear XYZ Automotive:

Thank you for your response dated xxx. I understand why according to company policy you would not be able to immediately make a decision to reimburse me for the 3,000 request for engine repairs. I believe I may have erred in not providing enough information for you to make that decision.

I failed to report that my car was in your shop for repair 2 years before the date of the engine repair. At that time, the odometer was supposedly fixed. As it turns out, I took it to another shop and they repaired it properly and told me that it actually had been set to "overstate" the mileage by 1,200 miles.

This means that actually my car was still under warranty when the engine repair was performed at your shop on xxx date. I have attached a PDF file as evidence of the dates and repairs.

Thank you for taking the time to consider carefully this new information. I would like to request a phone call within the next five working days. I can best be reached at 123-456-7890.

FIGURE 7 *Complete letter.*

4. Does the message pass the AIDA system test?

5. Did the message create good will?

Using a Problem, Solution Approach

If you are writing your appeal in the form of a problem and solution, you will want to create a shared goal with your reader. For example, a shared goal in the case of ABC Automotive would be for both customer and ABC to continue to do business together, so that they both leave feeling a sense of good will. Both client and service provider want to project a positive image of the company so that further services will be sought by the client as well as by other consumers.

The client in this case does need to be prepared, to prepare factual information, to have a legitimate business claim, and to be reasonable. In return, ABC needs to seriously, and in good time, determine if the client does have a legitimate claim; and, if so, how to respond. If they do not reimburse the client for the $3,000 repair bill and the client does have a valid case (they have done their research and the data are accurate), then it would not be in the best interest of ABC to refuse the reimbursement, even though it is a large sum of money. They will want to avoid a possible lawsuit, which could certainly cost much more than $3,000. They could also incur some very bad external public relations news about their company. This is a serious consideration with business, with the use of the Internet. There are sites like "Yelp," "Yahoo," and "Angie's List" that consumers visit on a regular and immediate basis to post their experiences with a particular company or service.

Hopefully, the negative direction that we have just outlined can be avoided, if both consumer and service provider see themselves as stakeholders in a mutual goal or problem where both benefit by a stated solution.

Summarizing the Plan for a Request

Whether presented as an "Explanation Request" with the end goal of persuading the reader, or as a "Problem Solution Request" with a shared goal, the request plan should follow these rules:

- Begin and end on a positive note. Avoid any kind of negative communication at the beginning and end of the message.

- Write with a "you-viewpoint." Consider the reader and write to the person's level and best interest.

- Use an indirect approach where you try to convince with details and facts.

- Be clear and concise and pay very careful attention to your word choice.

◾ Ask for action, respectfully and positively, showing a shared benefit where possible.

What to avoid:

Do avoid being selfish and blunt and using a direct approach. Do not assume you will get a negative reaction. Do not send a message that is poorly planned and delivered, as this is a lazy approach and your reader will know it.

Sales Messages

One of the most important and widely disseminated pieces of literature from a company is the sales message. Though you may not work directly in the sales field, you most likely will find yourself in a position of promoting your product or service, or even yourself. Whether you are in business or education; supporting a political, religious or ethical cause; or looking for employment, you will find yourself involved in the business communication process of writing and/or delivering a sales message.

Designing a sales message is a delicate balancing act. You need to balance the persuasive act and delivery of information with not being too invasive or direct. You want the message to be read, not rejected. You will want to grab the attention of the reader in a fashion that creates curiosity and engagement so that the reader is motivated to move from the initial attention-getter—whether it be a graphic, an opening line, or a catchy design—into the details of the product or idea that you are selling. Let your reader see the central idea of your message, see the benefit, and then act upon it.

Creating and Delivering the Effective Sales Message

A recent report by "JupiterResearch" shows that online advertising is outperforming previous expectations, and is to reach 9 percent of total ad spend by 2011 (www.marketingvox.com). Paid search is where the largest increases have been seen, with new keyword placement driving up prices. In addition, certain subsections of display advertising such as video and rich media will grow rapidly and begin to cannibalize static display advertising, the report concludes.

Jonathan Kantor believes that an interesting and powerful combination of advertising is found through using both the more conventional and highly regarded "white paper" in addition to social media (www.whitepapersource.com). The white paper, regarded in technical and government circles for its detail and validity, has emerged in the commercial world over the past 15 years as a common marketing tool. A white paper typically opens up with a problem or

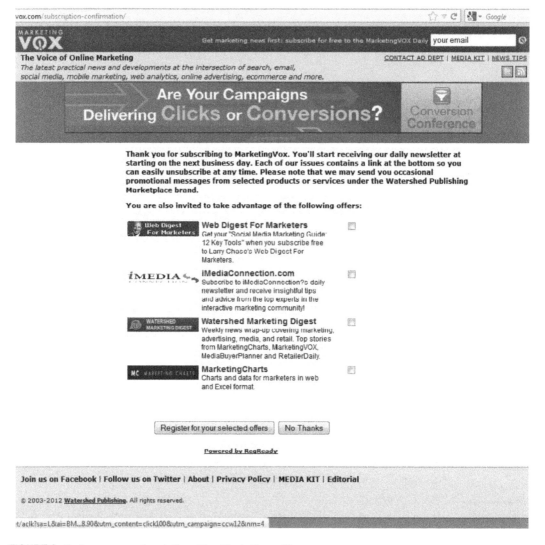

FIGURE 8 *Online news subscription, Vox Marketing with social media links. Printed with permission*

description of a situation that a company may soon face, and then it offers a solution to that problem. As Kantor states, it has the same white-hot status now as social media. Twitter, Facebook, and LinkedIn are no-cost vehicles to post a white paper and leverage peer exposure. Kantor goes on to state that great content, which is what is found in white papers, is what builds social media followers.

Although technology has changed the delivery method of a good sales message, the need for the message itself to contain good content has not changed. Good content requires good writing! What distinguishes the sales message from

FIGURE 9 *Online ads based on search terms.*

other forms of messages we have addressed is the strong persuasive approach and a focus on reiteration of a central message. The words in the sales message should be chosen carefully, accentuating the strengths of the product, service, or idea, and they should be crafted to gain attention, hold attention while the persuasive case is developed, and then ask for action. As with any good message, a "you-viewpoint" should be used and the tone should be positive and convincing. You need to be convinced, in order to convince the reader! Other helpful writing techniques are to use humor, variety, and emotion, while keeping the audience in mind.

© violetkaipa, 2012. Used under license from Shutterstock, Inc.

FIGURE 10 *Sales campaign brainstorming.*

Creating the Effective Sales Campaign

Beyond sending a single sales message, a company may want to create a more broad-based and longer-term sales campaign. This requires more extensive planning and execution. Many of the same principles of creating good content, and creating a message that is persuasive and compelling, are involved. Additionally, there are other more overarching considerations, as seen in the illustration below.

In Figure 5.10, we can see key elements by way of brainstorming, in the form of graphic sketches and key words that are part of planning an effective sales campaign.

Best Practices Planning Questions

- What is the **Central Idea?** State the central idea at the beginning of the message, repeat it in the middle, and reiterate it again at the end of the message.

- How much Money or **Profit** will this make? What is the anticipated net profit from the sales campaign?

- How much will it **Cost?**

- What is the **Timeframe?**

- **Where** will it be **Marketed**? New York City, Brazil? These are recognizable in the figure.

- What part of the reader's **Emotional Makeup** will this sales message be touching?

- What is the **Educational Level**, the **Family Makeup**, the **Income Level**, the **Value Set** of the target audience?

Keeping all of these factors in mind, an individual, or a team will create and present the sales campaign.

Presenting the Sales Message   At some point, the idea will need to be presented in a formal fashion. The most widely used presentation software used in marketing and sales presentation meetings is PowerPoint. The visual and multimedia power of this presentation software package is so effective that it has become a key skill to possess and apply in schools, businesses, and nonprofit organizations.

To create an effective sales presentation, it is important that the factors listed in Figure 9 have been considered and woven into the sales campaign. The excellent writing techniques discussed in Chapters 1 through 4 should be incorporated in the presentation. Finally, use an appropriate persuasive approach that fits your audience, so that it is well received.

© Kaspars Grinvalds, 2012. Used under license from Shutterstock, Inc.

FIGURE 11 *Business presentation.*

Social Media and Online Advertising and E-mail Marketing Campaigns

Online search engines collect information from people who "opt" to use their services, such as Gmail, Yahoo, and Hotmail Internet mail, as well as search engines such as Google, Bing, and Yahoo. While using these services, you may be asked to provide your e-mail address to visit a particular page, to receive a service, or to place an order. Now your e-mail address is linked to the Web search engine site you are visiting. If you provide your work e-mail, it is linked to the site where you are conducting the search or using the free online service. You may be shopping online, researching online, conducting online banking, or making reservations for a business or personal trip, all daily tasks that most of us engage in.

Consumers have become so accustomed to using these free online services, that they sometimes do not understand the need for companies offering the free services to support themselves through advertising, just as any company would. In Gmail, for example, algorithms read your mail and present ads at the side of the message in your inbox. It is important not to confuse online advertising with permission-based e-mail. Online advertising, targeted at the consumer, based on the data collected from your online use, is collected "behind the scenes." Permission-based e-mail gives the consumer a choice, is interactive, and highly effective. E-mail marketing is the most effective form of online promotion today according to emarketer.com (www.comf5.com) Potential customers may be given a list of products or services they can choose or "click on," thereby tailoring the ads to meet their needs. This type of e-mail is one of the most important contributing factors in successful marketing campaigns.

Most permission-based e-mail has a preset value of "opt-in," which means that you will receive the e-mail advertising automatically, but you can discontinue it by clicking on a link that allows you to "opt out" of receiving that e-mail advertising in the future. It is important to include these opt-out notifications in any kind of e-mail marketing campaign, so that consumers do not feel an invasion of privacy or feel forced into accepting e-mails that some might consider spam or unwanted mail.

Analyzing the Results

In an e-mail-based marketing campaign, results must be analyzed to see if the campaign was successful. An online sales campaign needs to employ companies that do the following: manage the large volumes of e-mail sent to multiple contact lists, track who opens your e-mails and when, and track the links that are clicked on. This type of tracking is referred to as Analytics. This service can also offer professionally designed templates, perform advanced queries regarding the segmentation of advertising, and provide data mining. Ultimately, these data help you continually redefine the marketing approach to reach and engage customers.

FIGURE 12 *"Results"—The final step.*

RFP Proposals

The Request for Proposal or RFP is a document issued to potential suppliers in a procurement process. Procurement is the acquisition of goods and services. The RFP brings structure to the bidding process and can often be used to flush out potential bidders who do not meet the qualifications of the RFP. Price, quantity, financial history, and product or service availability are examples of information that may be requested in an RFP. As you can imagine, due to the varying nature of business, products, and services, the content of RFPs varies widely, but the process and document itself is widely recognized and used in business, government, education, and non-profit organizations. Generally, the RFP is sent to an already established and recognized list of vendors.

After the RFP is disseminated, interested bidders return a Proposal to the Request For Proposal by a certain date and time. The receipt of the proposal often leads to discussions to clarify technical considerations, price, or other factors.

The Internet abounds with various sources for RFP templates and services. Current RFPs by city or department are often published on Websites that have extensive contact information and a searchable database, such as the Port of San Diego, at http://www.portofsandiego.org/business/view-current-rfprfbs.html and the Virginia Department of Transportation at VDOT at http://www.virginiadot.org/business/rfps.asp (RFP_CFXProfessionalServices.pdf). Often the documents are posted as PDF files. Note that the documents use bulleted items, tables, lists, graphs, and charts to organize the extensive data.

Example of a professional white paper "L-Soft," Email Marketing Best Practices.

Whitepaper

Email Marketing Best Practices

Winning Techniques for Today and Tomorrow

August 25, 2010
Copyright © 2010 L-Soft international, Inc.

FIGURE 13 *E-mail marketing best practice in the form of an online white paper.*
http://www.lsoft.com/resources/pdf/wp-E-mailMarketingBestPractices.pdf

Introduction

Many companies have turned to cost-effective online communication methods such as email marketing to reach and engage their customers. Looking ahead, companies will continue to invest in email marketing. According to well-established research companies such as Forrester and JupiterResearch, email marketing spending runs into the billions both in the United States and in Europe.

Implementing an effective email marketing communication platform involves multiple tasks, such as building a permission-based list of recipients, managing the list, defining relevant content in the right format, delivering the message and evaluating the results. With best email marketing practices, companies will experience the return on investment required to justify expenditures. With years of experience in the email industry, L-Soft can provide you with an introduction to email marketing and guidance on how this effective tool can benefit your company. The following pages feature facts, expertise, and guidance on key email marketing topics.

This white paper contains time-tested techniques and best practices that we hope you will find of value as you strive for success in your email marketing efforts. For more information about email marketing or L-Soft's products and services, please contact us at: info@lsoft.com. To keep up-to-date with the latest L-Soft news, visit our opt-in email list sign-up page at: http://www.lsoft.com/contact/optin.asp.

Fast Facts

- Marketers rate email to in-house lists as among the most effective forms of online advertising. According to the early-adopter online marketers, email marketing to in-house lists is among the top three best performing online advertising tactics. About a third of these marketers plan to increase the budget for email marketing to in-house lists with 5 percent or more in 2007. [1]

- Despite spam, almost 80 percent of consumers subscribe to receive messages from companies. Permission-based commercial email is relevant to a majority of customers. [2]

- 71 percent of U.S. online marketers have used email marketing in the past 12 months, and an additional 12 percent plan to use it within the next 12 months. [3]

- 45 percent of U.S. email users think that "e-mail is a great way for companies to stay in touch with customers". [4]

- Most B2C and B2B marketers expect the impact of email marketing to increase in 2007. [5]

- Sixty percent of marketers state that to "engage and build relationships with existing customers" is one of their primary reasons for using email marketing. [6]

- U.S. Internet users spend 15 percent of total Internet time one mail. [7]

- JupiterResearch forecasted in 2006 that email marketing spending will grow to $1.1 billion by 2010 in the United States. [8]

- According to Forrester, the value of the European email marketing market will grow by 12% per annum, hitting €2.3 billion in 2012. [9]

- Email has among the highest return on investment (ROI) index of all marketing channels. [10]

- According to marketers who measure their campaigns, 40 percent said email earns the highest ROI, followed by search (28 percent) and direct mail (18 percent). [11]

Email Marketing Benefits

Email is Inexpensive

Email is far less expensive on a cost-per-contact basis than other advertising options, including banner ads, print advertising, and telemarketing.

Email Creates Quick Response Cycles

Email cuts response times down from as much as six to eight weeks for direct mail to as little as 48 hours in most cases.

Email Marketing Campaign Results are Measurable

Campaign success can be measured using software designed to record responses or sales that are attributable to email marketing efforts. Reports can be generated on the number of emails opened by your recipients (open-ups) and the number of times your embedded links were clicked (click-throughs). By being able to quantify the success of campaigns while in progress, marketers can quickly adjust strategies to strengthen response rates.

Email Has Wide Reach

Email is the most widely used facet of the Internet and is part of many people's daily routine. It is a communication medium with an exceptionally large audience that allows recipients to immediately act on messages.

Email Drives Web Site Traffic and Registration

Email is an effective way of driving people to your Web site. Links may be embedded within messages, quickly directing customers to your site. With any luck, this increased Web site traffic will then lead to increased Web site registration. You may then follow up by providing your customers with personalized and targeted content.

Email Strengthens Brand Awareness and Builds Customer Relationships

Regularly delivered email messages that contain properly titled subject lines and logos reinforce company and product awareness. Email creates an interactive connection with customers and nurtures long-lasting, quality relationships.

Email Can Be Highly Customized

When email lists work together with customer databases, even large-volume campaigns can be customized so that messages include specific customer data. Database integration also allows select customer groups to receive messages appropriate for only a portion of database entries (for example, ZIP Code-, gender-, or income-based mailings can be easily selected and targeted for delivery).

Email Saves Time

Compared to traditional direct marketing, email marketing campaign administration is efficient and saves time and money.

Email is Easy to Implement and Requires Limited Resources

Email campaigns can be quickly implemented and executed with only minimal software, hardware and personnel investments.

Example of the Value of Email

Let's take into consideration this situation: Your company is planning to distribute a newsletter to customers, prospects, and other interested parties, and it is your job to decide how to accomplish this task. The monthly newsletter will contain many regular features, including articles, advice, and industry news. You have two options to distribute the newsletter: You can print the newsletter and snail-mail it to recipients - after all, this is how company newsletters have been distributed for many years. This is still an effective option, but have you considered the many benefits of sending your newsletter via email? In addition to saving costs (including paper, printing, and postage), email allows you to do things that you would not otherwise have been able to do if you chose print format.

If you choose to email the newsletter and select an advanced software program to manage the mailing, you will be able to measure what sections of the newsletter are most popular with readers. When you send an email newsletter, recipients click on embedded links to retrieve articles they wish to read. These clicks are measurable and provide you with valuable information that can, in turn, be used to tailor future newsletters to best suit readers' interests. However, if you choose print format to deliver the newsletter, there is very little you can do to quantify what portions of the newsletter are popular and are being read.

Email makes a difference. This is why more and more organizations and companies are turning to email to conduct marketing initiatives.

How to Use Email Marketing

As email has evolved, marketers have discovered clever ways to take advantage of its usefulness. Some common ways companies have integrated email into their communication efforts include:

- **Sending newsletters and building an online community Pearson Education (NYSE: PSO)**, which provides an online resource for technology information, uses LISTSERV® to manage more than 20 newsletters to subscribers about topics ranging from programming to networking. These newsletters have enabled Pearson Education to build a strong IT community that subscribers can depend on for up-to-date technology news.

- **Sending conference announcements, guides and tickets Stockholm International Fairs** is the leading exhibition and congress center in Scandinavia and the Baltic Sea region. In 2002, the company started using LISTSERV® Maestro to provide conference announcements, tickets, and pre-registration opportunities to exhibitors and attendees using email. Stockholm International Fairs has achieved campaign cost savings and improved information distribution to exhibitors and visitors. The number of conference registrations has also increased thanks to the mailings.

- **Sending announcements and improving communities United Way** is a national volunteer organization dedicated to bringing together communities across America. The organization incorporated ListPlex® Maestro into its operations to improve communication with staff, donors, volunteers and those interested in knowing more about their communities. A growing number of LISTSERV® lists have increased United Way's ability to gather available resources and improve communities across the country. Based on this successful foundation, the United Way is currently implementing L-Soft's email list services in its regional and local service centers.

- **Offering reminder services**; for example, in March 1999, Lifetime Television launched a campaign on its Website called the Lifetime Breast Self Examination Reminder Service to raise public awareness of breast cancer and the importance of early detection. Visitors to the site are given the opportunity to register for a free, monthly examination reminder through email. The company chose the LISTSERV® email list management software to deliver this health reminder to its subscribers. As Lifetime's needs have grown, today, the organization is using LISTSERV® Maestro. Its Breast Self Examination Reminder list has more than 77,000 subscribers. Since its launch, Lifetime TV has started nine other lists about topics ranging from its most popular television shows to special promotions and offers.

Database Integration

A unique advantage of email marketing is the ability to customize messages. This is achieved through integration with your customer database. By incorporating customer demographic information stored in your database, you are able to study customers' histories and buying habits in order to more effectively target and customize your messages. For instance, if you sellout door gear, you may configure your email marketing software to send offers for discounts on overstocked raingear to customers with zip codes in the Pacific Northwest, or likewise send those who reside in the deserts of Arizona similar offers on sunglasses.

Steps to a Successful Email Marketing Campaign

1. Gather a List of Subscribers

In order to begin any email marketing campaign, you must first compile a list of email addresses from those who have agreed to receive your messages. This is known as *opt-in*[1] email marketing and is a very important part of your campaign.

Building a quality permission-based email list will achieve more desirable results. Be upfront about how secure your subscriber's information is, whether or not you will be sharing that information with a 3rd party, and specific instructions on how your subscribers can opt out of your list. So, with those concerns out of the way, where do you begin? A logical place to start gathering addresses is with:

   a. **Current Customers** who may have previously provided you their email addresses and given you permission to send messages. Depending on how your business operates, there may be opportunities to collect your customers' email addresses through purchase orders or other forms. Or, perhaps email communication may already be the most common way you correspond with your clients, and therefore, a perfect opportunity exists to ask them if they would like to receive newsletters or other offers.

---

[1] Opt-in and opt-out are concepts that have been developed to identify two kinds of privacy mechanisms and adapted to permission email. The opt-out method of email marketing involves giving consumers the option of not receiving promotional messages after they have already received a message. Under this system, messages can be sent until an individual asks not to receive messages (i.e., the individual "opts out"). With the opt-in method, consumers do not receive promotional messages unless they have actively agreed to receive such messages. Under this system, email cannot be sent unless the individual has expressly given permission.

Today, email solution providers and consumer protection agencies recommend the double opt-in procedure as a further step to prevent unsolicited email messages. After a respondent checks the permission box, an automated email message is sent to the provided email address to certify that the person did in fact provide permission to receive email. The address holder must then respond, typically within a given time period, to receive future mailings. This process ensures that others cannot sign up unwilling third parties for membership through online forms.

b. **Prospective Customers** whose email addresses may be obtained through sign-ups on your Web site or in-store locations (known as **Point-of-Presence** collection). Advanced email list management software has the ability to interact with your Web site so visitors may automatically subscribe to newsletters without your having to perform this function manually.

A good method to encourage Web site visitors to sign up for your newsletter or be included in your list is to offer them something they would not otherwise receive without being a subscriber. For example, offer members incentives like special discounts, coupons, gift certificates or access to products before release to the general public. White papers are also an inexpensive means of showing recipients that your company is serious about its business.

2. **Develop the Content and Format of Your Message**

Messages should be crafted according to the results you wish to achieve. What are your goals for this campaign? Generating sales? Branding? Driving site traffic? Generally, you should create a strong message that reinforces your brand, describes your products or services and clearly establishes how customers should contact you. The subject line is possibly the most important element of an email message. Create a powerful subject line by combining an action phrase with a response-boosting incentive. An example of a good subject line would be:

```
SUBJECT: Last Minute Fare Specials for Weekend Getaway
```

At this point you may wish to consider in what format your message will be sent: text-only, HTML, or MIME/Multi-Part format.

HTML mail has the ability to strengthen your message by combining graphical images (like your company or brand logo) with text. Studies differ greatly whether HTML or text is more popular overall. Still, it is advisable to allow subscribers to choose their desired form at themselves. Recipient format preference can be stored in your database much like you would store other preference and demographic information.[2]

A **MIME** or **Multi-Part** specification is intended to allow you to send messages in both text and HTML format. The recipient's email program then displays the format it can best view.

3. **Getting Your Message Out**

As your email marketing operations evolve and your mailings grow in size, it will become apparent that the task is too complex and requires too much manpower for your current system to handle. Select software that is capable of managing your lists as they grow and can measure the effectiveness of your campaign. Your software should have the ability to automatically remove bounced or undeliverable email addresses from your list, as you may find the task of manually removing such addresses very time consuming and tedious.

a. **Message Format Testing**

After crafting your message, it is important to test it to make sure it displays properly in many common email clients. Set up your own accounts using popular commercial providers, such as AOL, Yahoo!, and Hotmail. Send yourself or your colleagues the test message to determine if formatting problems exist. This

---

[2] Please note that not all email recipients are capable of receiving or reading HTML messages. Furthermore, it is not recommended to "sniff," a questionable method that attempts to determine whether recipients are capable of receiving HTML email, as this procedure simply examines a computer's settings and not necessarily the program used to read email.

testing is particularly important if you are sending HTML mail. Ensure that your HTML message is viewable in all major email clients and that the HTML code is standards-compliant. Pay close attention to how images are rendered. This is particularly important now that many email clients automatically block all external images in the message viewer until the recipient clicks a button to explicitly allow them or adds the sender to the address book. If you are not technically savvy, it is advisable to consult your staff Webmaster or a professional in this field.

b. Scheduling Delivery

A valuable feature of advanced email marketing and email list management technology is the ability to schedule delivery for a specific time and date. This feature ensures that your message arrives in subscribers' inboxes at an opportune time. If you can determine whether you have a recipient's home or work email address, scheduled delivery becomes even more valuable. If you have a worldwide audience, use a time zone correction feature, available in sophisticated software programs, to properly place your message in inboxes during an appropriate time.

Marketers have generally been more successful when they schedule home users for weekend delivery, the time they are most likely to recreationally check their email. Likewise, scheduling deliveries to 'work' recipients Tuesday through Thursday has been shown to be more effective, to avoid overloaded Monday inboxes and distracted Friday employees.

4. Evaluate and Revise Your Campaign

For best results, create a pilot campaign that tests the effectiveness of your message on a select portion of your database. Measure the results from the trial, make adjustments and test another group. Refine your message until you feel comfortable enough to launch a full campaign.

Once you have sent your final message to recipients, you can begin to measure campaign results. Monitoring responses enables you to determine the quality of your recipient lists and the effectiveness of email content. Email marketing programs are capable of recording whether recipients opened up the message, and if they did, whether or not they clicked on the embedded links included. By being able to quantify these activities, you can measure the success of campaigns and, if necessary, make adjustments to achieve higher conversion rates. This is a key component of an email marketing campaign.

Issues to Keep in Mind

Spam

One of the most used words in the email marketing industry today is "spam," or unsolicited commercial email. Unfortunately, because email marketing is relatively inexpensive, unscrupulous culprits have flooded in-boxes with unwanted junk mail. There are several measures you can take to stem the tide of spam and stay clear of problems:

- Follow national laws regarding the use of commercial email.

- Use a recognizable domain that states your company or product name. Also use authentication standards such as SPF, Sender ID, and DomainKeys so that your recipients can verify that the message did originate from your domain.

- Avoid using CAPITAL letters, bombastic wording, or gratuitous punctuation such as exclamation points in the subject line of your message.

- Use clearly stated wording and action verbs to identify the objectives of your message to subscribers.

- Provide clear instructions about how a subscriber may opt out of membership.

- Refer to your local market's codes of conduct to assure that you follow the guidelines of email marketing. This is particularly necessary when operating in or sending messages to Europe.

Viruses

Nothing will bring your email operation to a grinding halt and generate more ill will from customers than inadvertently sending subscribers a computer virus. Preventing an accidental outbreak is quite easy; however, if you choose software with built-in virus protection and an attachment filter that scans all messages and attachments for viruses before they are sent to subscribers.

Privacy

One of the biggest advantages of email marketing is its ability to measure campaign effectiveness on the individual recipient level, unlike other advertising mediums such as print or television ads. However, your marketing objectives may not necessitate individual result gathering. Moreover, subscribers may not give their permission to perform such tasks, or your ability to do so may be curtailed by laws in certain jurisdictions. Therefore, it is important to understand what level of tracking procedures to implement in your campaign.

Personal Tracking involves associating each individual event (such as click-through or open-up) with the specific recipient who triggered it. If this method of measurement does not fit your marketing objectives, you may wish to choose **Anonymous Tracking** or **Blind Tracking**, which measure events but don't associate them with a specific recipient.

Do's and Don'ts of Email Marketing

Do:

- Know your national laws and local guidelines for email marketing and ensure that you follow them.

- Build your list internally, even if it takes time, so the quality of your recipient list remains at a high level.

- Keep an accurate audit of how your company received permission to contact the subscribers of the lists; keep in mind that some people forget they signed up to receive information.

- Make membership to your email deliveries valuable by offering deals that non-members cannot receive.

- Make sure that your company's name (or product name) is clearly identified in the domain name that appears in the "Sender" line of the email.

- Use clearly stated words that describe what you want customers to respond to in both the "Subject" line and the body of your message.

- Provide recipients with a clear way to contact you for more information, including telephone number and email address.

- Provide subscribers with clear instructions of how to be removed from future mailings.

- Plan mailings for specific, opportune times so subscribers are expecting your messages and are in a position to respond.

- Personalize messages with recipients' names and tailor them for different target segments.

- Choose software that can perform as your opt-in email lists grow, scan outgoing messages for viruses and measure the effectiveness of your campaign.

Don't:

- Send messages to those who did not request to receive information.

- Purchase or rent lists from brokers who are not reputable and who cannot provide current, verifiable double opt-in permission.

- Use exclamation points, capitalized letters, or other blatant marketing techniques that are synonymous with spammers.

- Send irrelevant offers to members of your database. For example, if you run an online travel agency, do not send special airfare incentives that originate from airports that do not correspond with the zip codes members have provided.

- Overload recipients with too many emails; only offer truly special deals.

- Cram too many messages into a single email or send large attachments that may clog subscribers' inboxes.

- Neglect to test messages, especially HTML messages. In particular, test how images are rendered in common email clients since many automatically block all external images in the message viewer until the recipient clicks a button to explicitly allow them or adds the sender to the address book.

- Rely on your email program's spellchecker. Always have colleagues proofread your message for spelling and grammatical errors.

- Sell or rent your email lists to other organizations unless you have been given explicit permission to do so.

- Expect that every campaign will be an immediate home run; crafting quality messages takes time and requires feedback.

Legal Aspects of Email Marketing

Over the last couple of years, both the United States and the European Union (EU) have adopted legislation that establishes requirements for those who send commercial email messages. Below is a summary of Federal U.S. and EU laws.

CAN-SPAM (United States)

The CAN-SPAM Act of 2003 (Controlling the Assault of Non-Solicited Pornography and Marketing) "covers email whose primary purpose is advertising or promoting a commercial product or service" (FTC Website, "Facts for Business"). The CAN-SPAM Act took effect on January 1, 2004.

- CAN-SPAM is based on the principle of opt-out. In other words, commercial email messages can be sent to a person until the individual explicitly asks to be removed from further mailings. Commercial email messages that are covered by the law need to include a return email address or other type of Internet-based response mechanism that allows the recipient to ask for further communications to cease. That request must be honored.

- It bans false or misleading email header information. The "From", "To", and sender information, including email address and originating domain name, must be accurate.

- It prohibits the use of deceptive subject lines to mislead the recipient about the content of the email message.

- Commercial email messages must include a clear notice that it is an advertisement or solicitation and that the recipient can unsubscribe (opt-out) from further communication. In addition, commercial email messages must also include the sender's physical postal address.

In the United States, there are also several state laws regarding commercial email messages. Where applicable, the federal law preempts state laws.

EC (European Commission) Directive on Privacy and Electronic Communication (EU)

As of October 31, 2003, all EU member states are covered by Article 13 in EU's Directive 2002/58/EC.

- EU's Directive on Privacy and Electronic Communication is based on the principle of opt-in. Email marketing messages can only be sent to natural persons (consumers) who have given their prior consent. However, there are several exemptions from the requirement of opt-in.

- If there is an existing customer relationship and said customer has not initially refused commercial contact via email, a seller of a product or a service has the right to market to the customer its own similar products or services. In this case, the sender has to offer the recipient a free-of-charge and an easy-to-use mechanism to say "no" to future emails.

- It is okay to send commercial messages to legal persons (business owners and employees) without prior consent. In this case, the sender also has to offer the recipient a free-of-charge and an easy-to-use mechanism to say "no" to future emails.

- It is prohibited to disguise or conceal the identity of the sender in a commercial email message.

- It is prohibited not to include a valid address to which the recipient can send a request that further communications cease.

Each member state has implemented the Directive into its national laws. Member states are entitled to impose stricter legislation than outlined in the Directive.

L-Soft's Approach to Addressing Email Marketing Legislation

L-Soft is an avid opt-in advocate. The single best advice L-Soft can give you to comply with email marketing legislation is to adopt an opt-in policy for all your commercial email deliveries, including business and consumer communication. We recommend our clients impose an opt-in-only approach. We think it is in the best interest of all parties, including sender and recipient. In addition to keeping you from breaking national opt-in laws, your organization will benefit from using opt-in by achieving increased responses and better results from your email marketing campaigns.

Tips on Complying with the U.S. Legislation & Building Trust with the Sender[3]

- Never give the recipient a reason to doubt who has sent the email by using vague or misleading sender information. Never use false headers to hide your true identity.

- Make it easy for recipients to get in contact with you. Include your office mailing address, telephone number and an email address that is monitored by a person.

- Don't mislead your recipients with subject lines that don't correspond with the actual content of the email.

- Make it easy to unsubscribe from your email deliveries by including an easy-to-use automated unsubscribe feature. Use a solution that automatically and directly removes the email address from your email list.

Tips on Complying with the European Union Legislation & Building Trust with the Sender[4]

- Ask for permission before sending commercial email messages to your customers. L-Soft recommends that you ask for permission for business-to-business communication as well.

- To avoid any national differences compared to the EC Directive, read the national law of the EU member state to which you are sending commercial email messages. The EC directive sets minimum levels on what countries must include in their national legislation, but they are free to set stricter rules.

- Always offer a free-of-charge and easy-to-use mechanism in each email you send to allow recipients to say "no" to future email messages.

- Never give the recipient a reason to doubt who has sent the email by using vague or misleading sender information. Never use false headers to hide your true identity.

- Make it easy for recipients to get in contact with you. Include your office mailing address, telephone number and an email address that is monitored by a person.

How Email Marketing Software Works

Although many marketers prefer to concentrate less on the technical side of email marketing and more on the content of the messages, it is important to have a basic understanding of how email marketing software works. In order to efficiently conduct an advanced email marketing campaign, it is essential to employ professional email list management software. The software must be installed on a server with a dedicated connection to the Internet. Your Web site and database then communicate directly with the software. When someone visits your company Web site and signs up to receive your newsletter, the software will automatically add the email address to an email recipient list for future mailings.

Your email list management software should have the ability to automatically handle all subscriptions and sign-offs as well as bounced email messages. The software should also be capable of connecting to your database and pulling out specific information about your

---

[3] See the next footnote.
[4] Disclaimer: The information provided is not intended and does not constitute legal advice. Please consult your legal team if you have questions and before conducting any type of email marketing activity.

recipients. This information can then be inserted into messages to create personalized mailings. More advanced software, capable of measuring campaign results, will provide your organization with better opportunities to strengthen your marketing efforts. The ability to track email responses is an important part of an email marketing campaign because it allows you to determine how effective your campaign has been. By being able to rapidly quantify results, marketers can make instant adjustments to their campaigns and achieve optimal results.

The average mail server cannot deliver the volume of email that you may one day require. The quality of your email delivery system determines the rate at which email is delivered. Your company may find it worthwhile to invest in faster and more robust email delivery software to guarantee that your email is delivered as efficiently as possible.

L-Soft offers advanced software and hosting services with the most up-to-date features and functions in the email industry. The company's **LISTSERV®**, **LISTSERV® Maestro**, and **HDMail** software products, and **ListPlex®** and **EASE^{SM}** hosting services keep more than 3,700 worldwide customers' email operations running smoothly and effectively.

How to Choose an Email Marketing Solution

By 2008, more than $6.1 billion will be spent on email marketing resources. [1] As the industry continues to grow, more and more vendors will offer products and services to satisfy the demand. How then can you be certain that your investment in email marketing software and services will be sound? Here are a few key questions to consider before you decide to purchase an email marketing solution:

1. **Will the Software Scale as My Needs Increase?**

   Most likely, one goal of your email marketing agenda will be to expand your list and perhaps create additional lists. If you purchase an email list management solution and maintain a single mailing list with 1,000 subscribers, the product may not have the capability to function when your success dictates that you run five lists with 10,000 subscribers each. Set realistic expectations for where your email marketing operation will be in one to two years from when you make the initial purchase, and determine whether the product will have the ability to handle the additional workload. Keep in mind that some software products can be purchased in increments and increased in capacity over time.

2. **Can the Software Be Integrated with Other Key Applications?**

   Imagine spending thousands of dollars on an email marketing solution only to find that it will not work in conjunction with your database or other key applications. If you have previously invested heavily in customer database capabilities, finding email marketing software that seamlessly integrates with your database will save time and money.

3. **Does the Vendor Offer Evaluation Kits?**

   Savvy IT professionals will evaluate a product on a trial basis before recommending it. Take advantage of the opportunity to evaluate email marketing software before purchasing to ensure that it performs as advertised.

4. **How Quickly Will I Be Up and Running?**

   Installing any new technology product should be as painless a process as possible. Often, businesses cannot afford to tie up resources for extended periods of time during installation procedures. Have your organization's technical staff review the product's installation manuals to determine how much time and resources will be required to install the software or find out if the company offers installation/configuration services.

5. Will the Vendor Be There for Me after Purchase?

Email marketing software is sophisticated, and often marketers find that they are not taking full advantage of every feature. Extended training courses may be necessary to ensure that your organization is getting the most out of its investment. Also inquire about the vendor's support policies, which should cover any technical difficulties you may encounter.

6. Does the Vendor Offer Both Licensing and Hosting Services?

Marketers often want to outsource their email marketing operations to companies that offer such services before bringing them in house. Outsourcing is a sound temporary solution, especially for small companies that may not have the hardware, personnel or capital to license software initially. This arrangement also provides a trial period for marketers to determine if the software is worthy of licensing, which is typically a more cost-effective solution in the long run.

7. Am I Getting My Moneys Worth?

Email marketing software and services are among the most cost-effective solutions your company will invest in. However, vendors vary greatly in price and the features they offer. Have a clear idea of what features and functions you demand, and evaluate many different products. Also determine whether licensing or outsourcing makes the best business sense for your company.

Outsourcing vs. Licensing

Before selecting a solution, you must evaluate which arrangement will best suit your needs: outsourcing or licensing. If you choose to license the software, you will conduct all operations on your premises. Without sourcing, email marketing operations (all functions except content creation) are hosted and run by another company that has expertise in that field.

OUTSOURCING vs. LICENSING		
	Outsourcing	**Licensing**
Benefits	• Smaller Investment of time. • Lower initial investment – no need to buy hardware or software. • Low human resource investment. • Quick setup.	• Increased control – the freedom to have complete control over the software and its functions. • Security – no risk to you that the vendor will go out of business or declare bankruptcy. • Messages may be sent according to your schedule. • Once you are regularly delivering a certain number of messages, it becomes more cost effective to license than outsource; ask your provider for a threshold number of messages that reflects the point at which licensing becomes more cost effective.

Requirements	• Personnel experienced with creating email marketing messages.	• Server hardware.
		• Appropriate bandwidth.
		• Proficient and experienced personnel capable of maintaining hardware and bandwidth requirements.
		• Personnel experienced with creating email marketing messages.
Limitations	• Less control over your campaign. • More expensive in the long run. • Dependency on your provider.	• Higher initial investment that is recovered if email traffic is large.

L-Soft's Email List Products and Services

LISTSERV® Email List Management Software

L-Soft's flagship product, LISTSERV®, developed by L-Soft founder and CEO Eric Thomas in 1986, was the first email list management software. LISTSERV® enables users to administer email lists of any size - from as many as several million subscribers to as little as a few. LISTSERV® is currently used to manage more than 425,000 lists and delivers about 35 million messages per day. The software is available for Windows 2003/2000/XP; Unix: AIX (PowerPC), Solaris (SPARC), Tru64, Linux (32-bit, 64-bit and S/390), AIX (PowerPC), HP-UX, Mac OS X; OpenVMS (Alpha), and VM. LISTSERV can connect to most ODBC-compliant (Windows and Unix) databases; Microsoft SQL Server; IBM DB2; ORACLE; and MySQL, allowing great flexibility with your choice of database.

LISTSERV® Maestro Email Marketing Software

LISTSERV® Maestro complements LISTSERV® and provides organizations with advanced software technology for conducting email marketing campaigns. LISTSERV® Maestro has an easy-to-use Web Interface that guides marketers through the steps of preparing email campaigns for delivery, including creating the message, assigning team responsibilities, selecting a targeted list of customers, testing and scheduling delivery, and tracking responses. LISTSERV® Maestro is available for Windows 2003/2000/XP; Unix (Linux 32-bit and Solaris on SPARC 32), and Mac OS X.

ListPlex® and EASE^{SM} Email List Hosting Services

ListPlex® and EASE^{SM} email list hosting services provide customers with access to L-Soft's expertise and technology without hardware, software, or personnel investments. Our outsourcing services can be tailored to meet the needs of the largest newsletters on the Internet, or simply help hobbyists keep in touch with others sharing the same interests.

ListPlex

Training and Consulting

L-Soft offers comprehensive training and consulting services to improve customers' effective and appropriate use of our electronic mail products and services. Our customized training services help you achieve your objectives quickly and efficiently by streamlining the learning process and eliminating the frustrating trial and error that often accompanies deployment of enterprise software. Training classes are hands-on courses that are tailored to meet the needs of your individual organization.

L-Soft also offers comprehensive consulting services, providing your organization with in-depth customized assistance throughout the implementation cycle. L-Soft's consultants can help integrate our products and services with your existing systems to more effectively address your email needs and to produce measurable business results. Through needs assessment, planning, implementation, testing, optimization and troubleshooting, L-Soft's consultants will guide you toward meeting your email objectives and achieving your business goals.

Contact Information

United States Office

L-Soft international, Inc.
8100 Corporate Drive, Suite 350
Landover, MD 20785-2231
USA

Phone: 1-301-731-0440
          1-800-399-5449

Sales: sales@lsoft.com

Press Contact: pressinfo@lsoft.com

European Office

L-Soft Sweden AB
Rosenlundsgatan 52, 2tr
118 63   Stockholm
Sweden

Phone: +46 (0)8-50709900

Sales: sales@lsoft.se

Press Contact: pressinfo@lsoft.se

United Kingdom Office (UK, Irish Customers Only)

L-Soft UK Ltd
Liberty House
222 Regent Street
London W1B 5TR
United Kingdom

Phone: +44 (0)207-2972007

Sales: uksales@lsoft.com

Press Contact: ukpressinfo@lsoft.com

Email Marketing Resources

If you wish to learn more about email marketing, L-Soft recommends these Internet sources of information:

LISTSERV® at Work

L-Soft's corporate newsletter that includes industry information, tips on how to conduct effective email communication and much more.

URL: http://www.lsoft.com/news/newsletter-us.asp (U.S.)

URL: http://www.lsoft.com/news/newsletter-eu.asp (EU)

ClickZ.com

The ClickZ network provides a massive resource center for all types of interactive marketing, including email marketing strategies and tactics.

URL: http://www.clickz.com

MarketingProfs.com

An online publishing company that specializes in providing marketing information, often through hands-on, know-how type of articles.

URL: http://www.marketingprofs.com

WordBiz Report

The newsletter of email and blogging by expert/consultant Debbie Weil.

URL: http://www.wordbiz.com/archive/index.html

eMarketer.com

eMarketer aggregates and analyzes research data about Internet business and marketing. They also publish a daily newsletter and reports on email marketing.

URL: http://www.emarketer.com/

MarketingSherpa

A media company with several newsletters that publishes various types of information, including case studies and articles, about Internet marketing.

URL: http://www.marketingsherpa.com/

Glossary of Terms

A

Above the Fold: The top part of an email message that is visible to the recipient without the need for scrolling. The term originally comes from print and refers to the top half of a folded newspaper.

Alias: A unique and usually shorter URL (link) that can be distinguished from other links even if they ultimately go to the same Web page. This makes it possible to track which message led viewers to click on the link.

ASP: Application Service Provider – A company that offers organizations access over the Internet to applications and related services that would otherwise have to be located on site at the organization's premises.

Attachment: An audio, video or other data file that is attached to an email message.

Auto-Responder: A computer program that automatically responds with a prewritten message to anyone who sends an email message toa particular email address or uses an online feedback form.

Authentication: A term that refers to standards, such as Sender ID, SPF, and DomainKeys/DKIM that serve to identify that an email is really sent from the domain name and individual listed as the sender. Authentication standards are used to fight spam and spoofing.

B

B2B: Business-to-Business – The exchange of information, products or services between two businesses – as opposed to between a business and a consumer (B2C).

B2C: Business-to-Consumer – The exchange of information, products or services between a business and a consumer – as opposed to between two businesses (B2B).

Bayesian Filter: A spam filter that evaluates email message content to determine the probability that it is spam. Bayesian filters are adaptable and can learn to identify new patterns of spam by analyzing incoming email.

Blacklist: A list containing email addresses or IP addresses of suspected spammers. Blacklists are sometimes used to reject incoming mail at the server level before the email reaches the recipient.

Block: An action by an Internet Service Provider to prevent email messages from being forwarded to the end recipient.

Bounces: Email messages that fail to reach their intended destination. "Hard" bounces are caused by invalid email addresses, whereas "soft" bounces are due to temporary conditions, such as full inboxes.

C

Challenge-Response: An authentication method that requires a human to respond to an email challenge message before the original email that triggered the challenge is delivered to the recipient. This method is sometimes used to cut down on spam since it requires an action by a human sender.

Click-Through Tracking: The process of tracking how many recipients clicked on a particular link in an email message. This is commonly done to measure the success of email marketing campaigns.

Click-Through Rate: In an email marketing campaign, the percentage of recipients who clicked on a particular link within the email message.

Conditional Blocks: A text fragment that is pasted into an email message only if certain conditions are met (for instance the recipient lives in a certain area). Conditional blocks allow email marketers to create more personalized mailings.

Conversion Rate: A measure of success for an email marketing campaign (for instance the number of recipients who completed a purchase). With email marketing, conversion rates are relatively easy to calculate because of the technology's measurable nature.

CPM: Cost Per Thousand – An industry standard measure for ad impressions. Email has a relatively low CPM compared to other marketing channels (Note: "M" represents thousand in Roman numerology).

D

Discussion Group: An email list community where members can obtain and share information. Every member can write to the list, and in doing so, everyone subscribed to the list will receive a copy of the message.

DNS: Domain Name Server (or system) – An Internet service that translates domain names into IP addresses.

DomainKeys/DKIM: DomainKeys/DomainKeys Identified Mail are cryptographic authentication solutions that add signatures to email messages, allowing recipient sites to verify that the message was sent by an authorized sender and was not altered in transit.

Domain Name: A name that identifies one or more IP addresses. Domain names always have at least two parts that are separated by dots (for instance, lsoft.com). The part on the left is the second-level domain (more specific), while the part on the right is the top-level domain (more general).

Domain Throttling: A technique that allows you to limit the number of email messages sent to a domain within a certain time frame. It is used to comply with ISPs and to avoid tripping spam filters. Many ISPs have their own policies and preferred limits.

Double Opt-In: The recommended procedure for subscribing email recipients to an email list or newsletter. Once a person requests to subscribe to a list, a confirmation email message is automatically sent to the supplied email address asking the person to verify that they have in fact requested to be included in future mailings.

E

Email Client: The software that recipients use to read email. Some email clients have better support for HTML email than others.

Email Harvesting: The disreputable and often illegal practice of using an automated program to scan Web pages and collect email addresses for use by spammers.

Email Header: The section of an email message that contains the sender's and recipient's email addresses as well as the routing information.

Email Marketing: The use of email (or email lists) to plan and deliver permission-based marketing campaigns.

F

False Positive: A legitimate email message that is mistakenly rejected or filtered by a spam filter.

Forward DNS Lookup: A Forward DNS Lookup, or just DNS Lookup, is the process of looking up and translating a domain name into its corresponding IP address. This can be compared to a Reverse DNS Lookup, which is the process of looking up and translating an IP address into a domain name.

FQDN: Fully Qualified Domain Name – A name consisting of both a host and a domain name. For example, www.lsoft.com is a fully qualified domain name (www is the host; lsoft is the second-level domain; and .com is the top-level domain).

G

H

Hard Bounces: Email messages that cannot be delivered to the recipient because of a permanent error, such as an invalid or non-existing email address.

Host Name: The name of a computer on the Internet (for example, www.lsoft.com).

HTML: Hyper Text Markup Language – The most commonly used coding language for creating Web pages. HTML can also be used in email messages.

I

In-House List: A list of email addresses that a company has gathered through previous customer contacts, Web sign-ups, or other permission-based methods. In-house lists typically generate higher conversion rates than rented lists.

IP Address: An IP (Internet Protocol) address is a unique identifier for a computer on the Internet. It is written as four numbers separated by periods. Each number can range from 0 to 255. Before connecting to a computer over the Internet, a Domain Name Server translates the domain name into its corresponding IP address.

J

K

L

List Broker: A company that sells or rents lists of email addresses. Some list brokers are not reputable and sell lists with unusable or unsubstantiated candidates. It is therefore advisable for email marketers to build their own internal lists.

List Owner: The owner of an email list defines the list's charter and policy (i.e. list description and general rules). The list owner is also responsible for administrative matters and for answering questions from the list subscribers.

M

Mail-Merge: A process that enables the delivery of personalized messages to large numbers of recipients. This is usually achieved using email list management software working in conjunction with a database.

Merge-Purge: The act of removing duplicate email addresses from a coalesced list that is composed of two or more existing lists.

MIME: Multi-Purpose Internet Mail Extensions – An extension of the original Internet email standard that allows users to exchange text, audio, or visual files.

Moderated List: Moderators must approve any message posted to an email list before it is delivered to all subscribers. It is also possible for the moderator to edit or delete messages. A moderated list puts the list owner in the equivalent position as an editor of a newspaper.

Multi-Threading: A process though which a mail server can perform multiple concurrent deliveries to different domains, which greatly speeds up the delivery of large volumes of email.

Multipart/Alternative: A message format that includes both text and HTML versions. Recipients can then open the message in their preferred format.

N

O

ODBC: Open Data Base Connectivity – A Microsoft standard for accessing different database systems from Windows, for instance Oracle or SQL.

Open-Relay: Open-relay is the third-party relaying of email messages though a mail server. Spammers looking to obscure or hide the source of large volume mailings often use mail servers with open-relay vulnerabilities to deliver their email messages.

Open-Up Tracking: The process of tracking how many recipients opened their email messages as part of an email marketing campaign. Open-up tracking is only possible using HTML mail.

Open-Up Rate: The percentage of recipients who have opened their email messages. The open-up rate is often used to measure the success of an email marketing campaign.

Opt-In: An approach to email marketing in which customers must explicitly request to be included in an email campaign or newsletter.

Opt-Out: An approach to email marketing in which customers are included in email campaigns or newsletters until they specifically request not to be subscribed any longer. This method is not recommended and may in some cases be illegal.

Out-of-Office Replies: Automatic email reply messages triggered by incoming email to a user's inbox, typically activated when users are on vacation or otherwise unavailable through email for an extended period.

Outsourcing: An arrangement where one company provides services to another company that would otherwise have been implemented in-house (See also "ASP").

P

Pass-Along: An email message that gets forwarded by a subscriber to another person who is not subscribed to the list (See also "Viral Marketing").

Personalization: The insertion of personal greetings in email messages (for instance "Dear John" rather than the generic "Dear Customer"). Personalization requires sophisticated email list management software that allows for so called mail-merge operations.

Plain Text: Text in an email message that contains no formatting elements.

POP: Post Office Protocol – A protocol used to retrieve email from amail server. Most email clients use either the POP or the newer IMAP protocol.

Q

Query: A subset of records in a database. Queries may be used to create highly specified demographics in order to maximize the effectiveness of an email marketing campaign.

R

Reverse DNS Lookup: A Reverse DNS Lookup is the process of looking up and translating an IP address into a domain name. This can be compared to a Forward DNS Lookup, which is the process of looking up and translating a domain name into its corresponding IP address.

Rich Media: An Internet advertising term for a Web page that uses graphical technologies such as streaming video, audio files, or other similar technology to create an interactive atmosphere with viewers.

S

Scalability: The ability of a software program to continue to function smoothly as additional volume or work is required of it.

Sender ID: Sender ID is an authentication protocol used to verify that the originating IP address is authorized to send email for the domain name declared in the visible "From" or "Sender" lines of the email message. Sender ID is used to prevent spoofing and to identify messages with visible domain names that have been forged.

Server: A program that acts as central information source and provides services to programs in the same or other computers. The term can either refer to a particular piece of software, such as a WWW server, or to the machine on which the software is running.

Signature File: A short text file that email users can automatically append at the end of each message they send. Commonly, signature files list the user's name, phone number, company, company URL, etc.

SMTP: Simple Mail Transfer Protocol – A protocol used to send email on the Internet. SMTP is a set of rules regarding the interaction between a program sending email and a program receiving email.

Sniffing: A method of determining whether or not email recipients are capable of receiving HTML-formatted messages. This procedure is not recommended as it is flawed and may result in inaccurate findings.

Soft Bounces: Email messages that cannot be delivered to the recipient because of a temporary error, such as a full mailbox.

Spam: (Also known as unsolicited commercial email) – Unwanted, unsolicited junk email sent to a large number of recipients.

SPF: Sender Policy Framework – An authentication protocol used by recipient sites to verify that the originating IP address is authorized to send email for the domain name declared in the "MAIL FROM" line of the mail envelope. SPF is used to identify messages with forged "MAILFROM" addresses.

Spoofing: The disreputable and often illegal act of falsifying the sender email address to make it appear as if an email message came from somewhere else.

Streaming Media: Audio and video files transmitted on the Internet in a continuous fashion.

Subject Line: The part of an email message where senders can type what the email message is about. Subject lines are considered important by email marketers because they can often influence whether a recipient will open an email message.

T

Targeting: Using demographics and related information in a customer database to select the most appropriate recipients for a specific email campaign

Tracking: In an email marketing campaign, measuring behavioral activities such as click-throughs and open-ups.

U

URL: Uniform Resource Locator – The address of a file or Web page accessible on the Internet (for example, http://www.lsoft.com).

V

Viral Marketing: A marketing strategy that encourages email recipients to pass along messages to others in order to generate additional exposure.

Virtual Hosting: A Web server hosting service that replaces a company's need to purchase and maintain its own Web server and connections to the Internet.

Virus: A program, macro or fragment of code that causes damage and can be quickly spread through Web sites or email.

W

White List: A list of pre-authorized email addresses from which email messages can be delivered regardless of spam filters.

Worm: Malicious code that is often spread through an executable attachment in an email message.

X

XML: Extensible Markup Language – A flexible way to create standard information formats and share both the format and the data on the World Wide Web.

Y

Z

References

[1] Ad:tech and MarketingSherpa end-of-the-year survey, January 2007, eMarketer, "What Works, and What Doesn't, in Online Marketing," http://www.emarketer.com/Article.aspx?id=1004532&src=article1_newsltr

[2] Forrester Research, "The State of Email Marketing 2004," March 26, 2004

[3] JupiterResearch sponsored by Kanoodle, "Kanoodle Content Targeting Survey," February 2005

[4] eMarketer, "E-Mail Marketing: How to Improve ROI", May 2005

[5] MarketingSherpa, Top Email Marketing Opportunities for 2007, http://www.marketingsherpa.com/article.php?ident=29823

[6] MarketingProfs.com, "Email Marketing Benchmark Survey 2004, "http://www.marketingprofs.com/downloads/MPEmailBenchmark2004.pdf

[7] ComScore, comScore Media Metrix, April 2004

[8] Forrester Research, European Email Marketing Spend Hits €2.3 Billion In 2012," http://www.forrester.com/Research/Document/Excerpt/0,7211,43165,00.html

[9] JupiterResearch, "JupiterResearch Finds Spam Is Shrinking While Email Marketing Is Growing Modestly," February 2006, http://www.jupitermedia.com/corporate/releases/06.02.03-newjupresearch.html

[10] Direct Marketing Association, "The DMA's 2003 Response Rate Study," "E-Mails Sent To House Files Found To Produce Highest Return-On-Investment For Soliciting Direct Orders," October 2003, http://www.thedma.com/cgi/disppressrelease?article=518

[11] MarketingProfs Email Marketing Survey, November 2005, From: Internet Statistics Compendium, July 2007, e-Consultancy,

REQUEST
FOR
PROPOSAL

PROFESSIONAL ENGINEERING SERVICES
for
Project Management
of the
Coalfields Expressway (CFX)
&
Route 460 Phase II Project

Bristol District

FIGURE 14 *Example of RFP, Virginia DOT.*

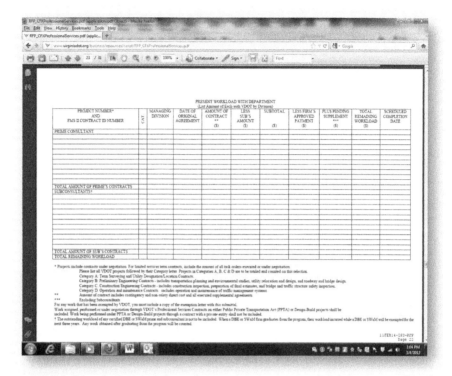

FIGURE 15 *Use of table in RFP.*

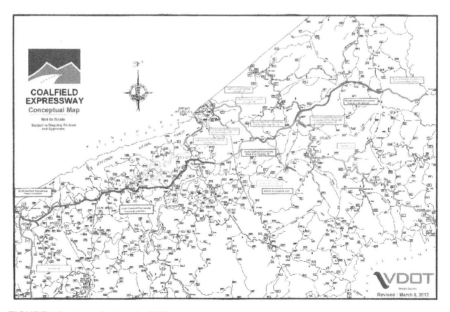

FIGURE 16 *Use of chart in RFP.*

The Report Cycle and the Use of Technology to Enhance Reports

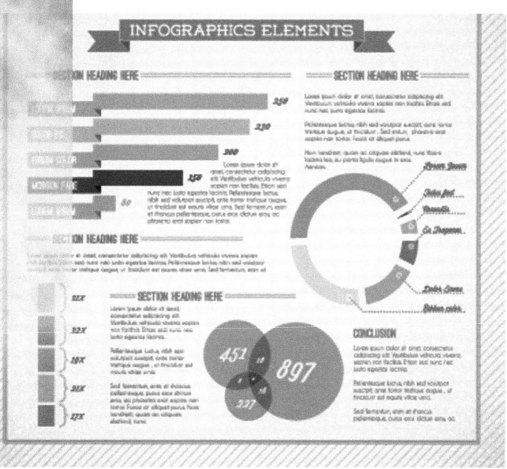

Chapter Five

Learning Objectives

LO1 Describe the Report Cycle.

LO2 Create graphs and charts to enhance a report and show significant data.

LO3 Describe options for adding formatting, color, and graphics to reports.

LO4 Identify MLA and APA document formats.

LO5 Compose a message that builds Good Will.

LO6 Describe the elements of a short report.

LO7 Describe the parts of a long report, including references and citations.

LO8 Describe various research methods.

LO9 Describe primary and secondary data.

LO10 Compose and present: a business proposal, a short research paper in a White Paper format and an accompanying PowerPoint presentation.

The Report Cycle

Reports are a form of business communication that are written to provide more information related to a problem or purpose. They are a form of direct communication and flow in an upward direction in the organizational hierarchy. With less face-to-face time in business, the globalization of the economy via technology, and more reports and data being transmitted via e-mail, the business report is becoming an increasingly important piece in effective communications and thus organizational success. Also, due to technology, there is much flexibility in how to write a report and what type of report to generate, but there are some common guidelines that will help you determine the following key factors when requested to write a business report. First, we will examine the cycle of report writing, in stages. Then we will consider different types of reports and their components.

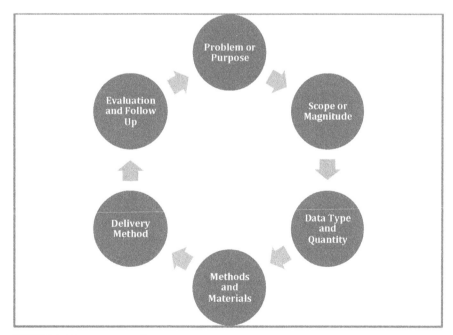

FIGURE 1 *The report cycle.*

The various stages of the business report cycle develop in much the following manner.

1. Problem or Purpose

Just as it is important to define a mission statement or an overarching purpose for an organization, it is important to define carefully the problem or purpose of a report. Effective writing, as we have stated previously, occurs when there is an accurate assessed need or purpose. Keeping the "you" viewpoint in mind and knowing the audience that will receive the report are very important in this stage.

2. Scope or Magnitude

Once the overarching purpose has been identified, the scope or magnitude of the report is defined. For example, based on the purpose, which parts of the organization, or perhaps a geographical area, need to be included? Often the scope will determine the type of report to generate—whether it is a long or short report; or a formal or informal report.

3. Data Type and Quantity

The scope or magnitude of the report dictates the type of data that need to be gathered. In turn, the type and quantity of data will determine the methods needed to collect the data and/or materials.

4. Methods and Materials

How will the data be collected? Using what processes, what forms, what materials? These items should be spelled out in a very detailed fashion, as they will determine the budget for the project.

5. Delivery Method

How will the report be delivered? It is important to determine how the report will be delivered. If it is an internal report, it may simply be delivered via in-house or internal e-mail. If the report is to be prepared for a client outside the company, an external report may be prepared in PDF format as a white paper or posted to a Website and delivered via e-mail. If the report is in the form of a proposal or a bid, it may need to be in prepared in hard copy format with signatures to be legal.

6. Evaluation and Follow-Up

Once the service or work is finished, it is important to perform an evaluation and follow-up on the feedback from the client. Remember, psychologically it is better to deliver more than what was promised rather than less, or to try to deliver as close to the target goal as possible. Evaluation and follow-up also give the sender(s) the chance to adjust their procedures for the next client, having learned from and adjusted their behavior from the previous job.

Report Format

There are many different types of report formats to choose from, and, as we discussed earlier, the scope or magnitude of the report as well as company or organizational standards, will often dictate the format. However, emerging technologies and the use of templates have made some elements very standard parts of any report or form.

Use of Technology to Enhance Reports

These standard elements that format and open well across many platforms, software applications, and browsers include the following. Use bullets, numbering, outlining, indentations, and tables for organization. Add charts and graphs, and built-in shapes to quantify data or to show trends and processes, and use built-in styles and templates to apply color and graphic shapes and designs.

Subheadings are also an important organizational aspect of report writing that chunks related data and standardizes the look of the document. Levels of subheadings are often shown in bold print and sometimes capitalized. They do not usually go beyond three levels, though more levels do exist. These subheadings then appear automatically in the table of contents.

The author kept this chart simple for easy visualization, with only two text-based labels and two numerical or quantitative data points. Charts become much more complicated, of course, given larger sets of data, which is typical in the business arena. However, the more you can simplify the data the better, so each component of the graph or chart displays itself, so to speak, and is an accurate representation of the numerical data.

The Visual Display of Quantitative Information, by Edward Tufte, is touted as "The classic book on statistical graphics, charts, tables.... with detailed analysis of

To organize:

➢ *Numbering*

1)

2)

3)

➢ *Outlining*

(i)

(ii)

(iii)

➢ *Indentations*

➢ 1)

o 2)

▪ 3)

➢ *Tables*

Numbering
Outlining
Indentations
Tables

FIGURE 2 *Built In organizational elements.*

FIGURE 3 *Use of subheadings.*

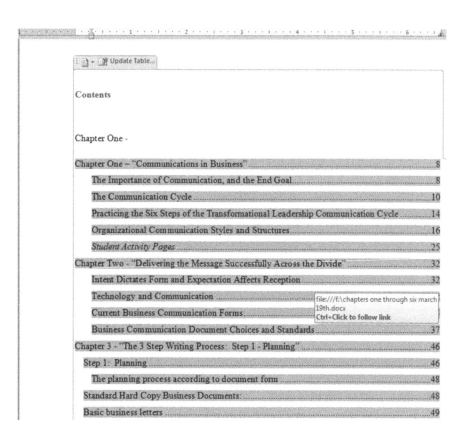

FIGURE 4 *Subheadings as captured in the table of contents.*

To quantify data or see trends and processes

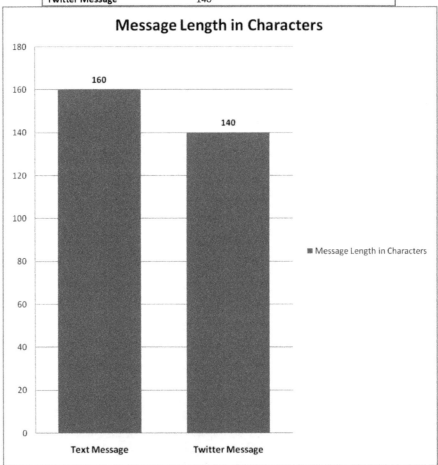

Social Network Media	
Text Message	160
Twitter Message	140

FIGURE 5 *Simple comparison bar chart.*

how to display data for precise, effective, quick analysis" (http://www.edwardtufte. com). His text booklet "Visual and Statistical Thinking" reprints Chapter Two of *Visual Explanations* and deals with such topics as displays of evidence used to decide the launch of the space shuttle *Challenger*. Yet another chapter discusses how PowerPoint templates typically weaken verbal and spatial reasoning and corrupt statistical analysis. (http://www.edwardtufte.com/tufte/books_pp)

Further, one of the primary responses that educators receive from industry regarding what skills they would like to see new hires possess is the ability to take meaningful company data and convey it concisely in speech, and precisely and clearly in graphic presentations.

To Apply Color and Graphic Design

Themes and styles are two rather new functions in word processing software that allow a document to have formatting "brushed" or selected and painted, if you will, across a series of sentences or paragraphs, or an entire document. With a few simple clicks of the mouse, one can transform a rather average looking document into a professionally formatted communication that has an appropriate amount of design and color to visually organize and lend consistency to a document's appearance.

Two choices that allow us to accomplish this are the Styles and Themes functions in the accompanying examples in Microsoft Word. "Styles" affect a portion of the document that has been selected, while "Themes" apply a stylistic format, professionally designed, to the entire document. After applying formatting to the entire document, sections can also be manually selected and formatted to change font, color, or effects, but it is advisable to use the majority of built-in functions in their existing state, and to not alter them too much, as they have been designed by professionals who specialize in graphic design and layout.

Styles affect text that has been selected for a particular level of heading. These changes are maintained when the document is saved in other formats, such as a Web page, as a PowerPoint presentation or a printed Publisher document and can even come across well when sent in the body of an e-mail.

Themes affect the entire document: titles, subtitles, font choice, colors for lines, borders, and other graphic features that the document may contain.

In the examples below, we will see the normal paragraph above with subheadings written in MLA style with no formatting applied, followed by an example of the text with Styles and a Theme applied.

FIGURE 6 *Styles in Word.*

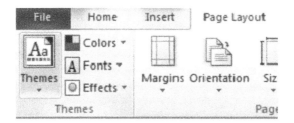

FIGURE 7 *Themes in Word.*

With the default "Office" theme, before the "Composite" theme is applied:

To organize:

> ➤ *Numbering*

  1)

  2)

  3)

> ➤ *Outlining*

  (iv)

  (v)

  (vi)

> ➤ *Indentations*

> ➤ 1)

  o 2)

   ▪ 3)

> ➤ *Tables*

Numbering

Outlining

Indentations

Tables

After the "Composite" Theme is Applied:
Do you see the differences below?

To organize:

> *Numbering*

    1)

    2)

    3)

> *Outlining*

    (vii)

    (viii)

    (ix)

> *Indentations*

> 1)

    o 2)

        ▪ 3)

> *Tables*

Numbering

Outlining

Indentations

Tables

FIGURE 8 *Comparison of data saved without a Theme applied and with a Theme applied.*

In addition to keeping these important organizational and graphic elements in mind for all report writing, it is equally important to maintain balance between flowing paragraphs that introduce, explain, and summarize material and the bulleted and tabled items that give emphasis to shortened points of data. Keep the readers moving with logical smooth transitions that take them from one piece of data, thought, or evidence to the next.

The example below incorporates elements of both a report and a form and uses many of the features of Word that make the document look clean, organized, and professional. It was created from a free source **template**, which can be accessed using the **File**, **New**, **Reports** command string in Microsoft Word. Then a **Theme** from the **Page Layout** menu was applied. These templates, using

FIGURE 9 *Templates in word processing software, Microsoft Word.*

[Type the company name]

[Type the document title]

[Type the document subtitle]

Author

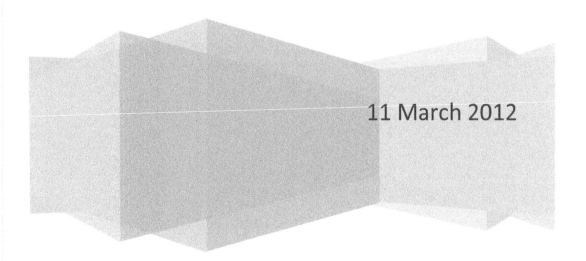

11 March 2012

FIGURE 10 *Example of Project Management Report/Form saved in PDF format.*

Project Name: xxxx   **Customer Name: xxxx**
Document Number / Version Number: xxxx

Checkpoint Report

1. Purpose

To report the status of work over a period by either an individual or a team, Checkpoint Reports are produced at a frequency defined in the Stage Plan and/or Work Package.

2. Derivation

The Checkpoint Report may be derived from the following:-

- Work Package
- Team Plan and actuals
- Previous Checkpoint Report

3. Quality criteria

What makes an Excellent Checkpoint Report?

- Prepared at the frequency required by the Project Manager
- The level and frequency of progress assessment is right for the stage and/or Work Package
- The information is timely, useful, objective and accurate
- Every product in the Work Package, for that period, is covered by the report
- Includes an update on any unresolved issues from the previous report

4. Tailoring

It is a principle that at PRINCE2 project tailors the method to suit its needs. Tailoring refers to the appropriate use of PRINCE2 on any given project, ensuring that there is the correct amount of planning, control, governance and use of the management products.
You may find it necessary to tailor this template up or down to meet the needs of your project. For everyone involved in the project, it should remain clear as to what the purpose of this management product is, what it should comprise and what the quality criteria are.
This template could quite easily be reduced to a 2 or 3 page document if required

Project Name: xxxx   **Customer Name:** xxxx
Document Number / Version Number: xxxx

5. Date

Sunday, March 11, 2012

6. Reporting Period

The reporting period covered by the Checkpoint Report.

7. Follow up and Evaluation

From previous reports, for example, provide a brief synopsis of progress on work allocated to you since you last submitted a checkpoint report. Highlight any issues, risks or actions you wish to bring to the project manager's attention.

Project Name: xxxx

Document Number / Version Number: xxxx

Customer Name: xxxx

8. This reporting period

The products being developed by the team during the reporting period.

Developed Products	Planned Date	Forecast date

The products completed by the team during the reporting period.

Completed Products	Planned Date	Completed Date

Quality management activities carried out during the period.

Quality Identifier	Product Identifier	Product Title	Dates	Results

Lessons identified.

Lesson Type	Lesson Detail	Logged By

9. Next reporting period

The products being developed by the team during the next reporting period.

Developed Products	Planned Date	Forecast date

The products to be completed by the team during the next reporting period.

Completed Products	Planned Date	Forecast Date

Quality management activities to be carried out during the next period.

Quality Identifier	Product Identifier	Product Title	Dates	Results

Project Name: xxxx   **Customer Name:** xxxx
Document Number / Version Number: xxxx

10. Work Package tolerance status

Tolerance	Element	Actual	Forecast	Variance
Work Package	Time			
	Cost			

11. Issues and Risks

Ref	Item	Description and update

Type: PI – Project Issue; RFC – Request For Change; OS – Off-specification; R – Risk

Project Name: xxxx   **Customer Name:** xxxx
Document Number / Version Number: xxxx

12.   Supporting Information

[Add here any supporting information, such as comments, charts, tables, documents or diagrams that will assist].

13. Checkpoint Report Sections Omitted

- [Omitted section]
- [Omitted section]

14. Document Distribution

Name	Organization	Role

15. Approvals

Prepared By   _____

([Job Title])

This document requires the following approvals

Approved By   _____

                   ([Job Title])

                   _____

                   ([Job Title])

Approval Date _____

various themes and colors, were designed by professionals, and they often are an excellent starting point for you to customize your own project or organizational needs. Figure 6.10 is a Project Management form template. A template is a read-only document that makes a copy of itself when opened, and is meant to be tailored to the organization's needs. Newsletters and quarterly or annual reports are examples of these templates. They are time saving devices for any organization, as the common elements, such as formatting, subheadings, signature lines, page numbers, headers, and footers, remain the same. Only the dynamic data, or data that change, need to be updated on a regular basis.

Short Reports

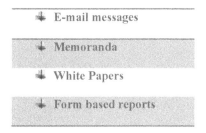

E-mail messages, memoranda, and form-based reports are examples of short reports. They may also include shorter white papers, approximately five pages or less. These reports should follow the same reporting processes and strategies as longer reports, but they do not require as much planning, as they are not as large in scope; therefore, they often do not require as much supporting documentation. We have seen examples of e-mail messages and memoranda in previous chapters.

Form reports have fields that one can tab or "mouse" to. Forms require specific data in certain locations and, if well developed, can save time. Company forms are often located on the internal organizational Website and can be downloaded and printed as hard copies or completed as fillable PDF forms. Fillable PDF forms are a staple in all sectors of business and government. These very popular forms are downloaded or saved, and then the interactive fields in the form itself are completed and often sent to the recipient via e-mail. Because this format opens independently of operating systems, applications, or hardware, it is considered open standard and is a universal file format. In fact, the PDF format was released as an open standard on July 1, 2008 (http://en.wikipedia.org/wiki/Portable_Document_Format) and is an ISO standard as well.

Given that the PDF format is universal, it is critical to understand how to send as well as receive PDF files. PDF files are "read-only" files, unless you have the entire Adobe Acrobat Writer© program, not just the free downloadable reader software, to read and open it in a non-read-only format so that the contents can be changed.

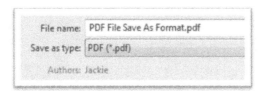

FIGURE 11 *File, Save As, dialogue box in Word, Save As PDF, or Portable Document Format*

FIGURE 12 *Adobe logo.*

Formal Reports

Depending on the need or the goal of the report, especially for a purpose that has a large scope, it may be appropriate or necessary to write a longer, formal report. The degree of formality tends to increase with the length of the document.

A formal business report, over a few pages, often contains a Title Page, a Table of Contents (TOC), perhaps a Table of Figures, and the Body of the report itself, which includes an Introduction, Supporting Paragraphs, and a Summary or Conclusion. A longer report also includes References, an Appendix, and an Index. The more involved the report is, the more parts it will include.

Title Page
The title page includes a meaningful title, the date of the publication, the author's name and title, and the organization or business name. Avoid excessively long

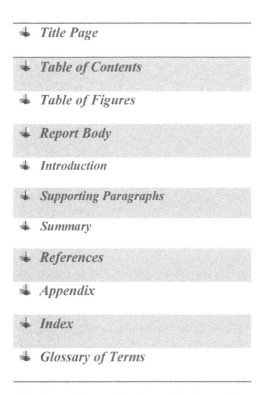

FIGURE 13 *Parts of the Formal Business Report.*

titles and instead use descriptive titles that represent the content of the report in a concise but comprehensive manner.

Table of Contents

The table of contents is a list format that provides the reader with information on the main headings and subheadings of the text with accompanying page numbers. It provides a preliminary order for the reader who is looking at the overall content of the report, as well as allowing the reader to refer to a specific section. There is a built in function in word processing software that updates the TOC as the writer adds to the report, adjusting the page numbers as information is added to or deleted from the report.

Table of Figures

Figures are an important element in a report. They illustrate particular data, photos, illustrations, charts, graphs, and trends. Often they will be contain a "Figure" caption, referred to as "**Figure x.x**" with the chapter number followed by the figure number of that chapter.

Body of Report Text

The report text includes the introduction, the body, and the summary of the report.

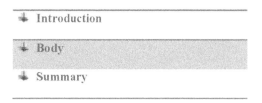

FIGURE 14 *Parts of body for Report Text.*

Introduction

The introduction of the report orients the reader to the problem and contains the main topic of the report. It is also common for the introduction to include why the report is being written, who the audience is, the scope of the report or research, and where the information was obtained, and it may introduce the topics in the main body of the report, in their order of appearance. It prepares the reader for what is to come and can also engage the reader by creating interest.

Body

The body of the formal report contains main ideas that were introduced in the opening paragraphs in much more detail. In the body of the report you are developing the argument, the position, and the problem, and then stating the resolution. You are using supportive evidence for the claims that you make or research that you are presenting. Use the same good writing techniques discussed in previous chapters. Introduce paragraphs in a logical, developmental order; use introductory and transitional phrasing and a smooth writing style. Be consistent and concise and prefer short sentences to long ones.

The body of the report may very well contain graphical elements illustrated in figures in previous pages of this chapter, such as Excel charts, graphs, and pivot tables, enumerated and tabled items, hyperlinks referring to sites on the Internet, and citations and footnotes, citing sources for the information that you have gathered.

Summary

The summary ties many things together from the introduction and main paragraphs. Here, the author summarizes the data, takes a position regarding the evidence and development of the argument in the main body, and/or states a resolution to the problem or situation that has been developed. It is important to write a strong summary and not leave the reader feeling as if there is something more that needs to be included, or more research that needs to be presented, or that the resolution or position that the author is purporting is not clear. Often in a formal business report or research report, the summary can include a call to action or next steps.

References

References follow the summary of the document. They can also be referred to as Works Cited or Bibliography. The style of the citations depends on the style of the report. An in-text parenthetical citation means that the author and date appear within the body of the text at the reference itself. If the report includes endnotes rather than in-text citations, the End Notes will precede the references.

Appendix

An appendix may be included if there is supplementary information related to the report, but the information is too long for inclusion in the report itself. If there is more than one Appendix, then list them as Appendix A, Appendix B, Appendix C, and so on, with a capital letter used for both the Appendix and its alpha designation. For example, for a full list on proofreading marks, see Appendix A, "Proofreader's Marks" or for a full list of white papers on e-mail marketing campaigns see Appendix B, "E-mail Marketing Campaigns White Papers."

Index

The index contains an alphabetical listing of the subjects by page number. The index is invaluable in a longer document so that the reader can go back and reference a particular page number, when remembering a topic that he or she would like to revisit. Word processing software makes it easy to update an index, as with each page addition or deletion page numbers are automatically renumbered.

Glossary of Terms

Alphabetized glossaries of terms and their meanings in reference to the report can be included. It is now common to see formal reports published to the Internet containing glossaries of terms that also contain hyperlinks to other sections of the report.

Outlining the main and subtopics of your report cannot be stressed enough. It is an important logical step in preparing and presenting your data, and it will keep you on track when writing.

The outline feature in word processing programs is an automated way to create your outline.

FIGURE 15 *Outline feature in word processing software.*

Referencing Methods In-text parenthetical citation styles include the American Psychological Association (APA), a scientific and professional style that represents psychologists, and the Modern Language Association (MLA), which is an organizational style that represents teachers and scholars on the formal and long end of the spectrum. Another style is a Business Report, which meets a business need, with length dictated by need, among other factors. An excellent guideline for writing in general, as well as for using MLA or APA formatting, can be found online at the Owl Purdue Online Writing Lab http://owl.english.purdue.edu/owl/resource/747/01/. Also, consult the latest version of the *MLA Handbook for Writers of Research Papers*. These styles are also included in word processing software with features

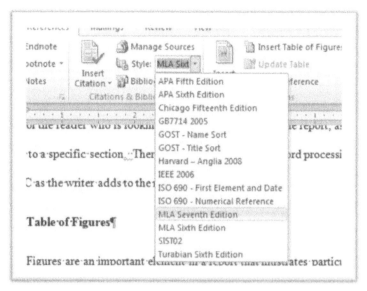

FIGURE 16 *Document style built into Word.*

that allow the writer to enter citations and footnotes manually, and with a feature that formats and manages both the sources and the bibliography.

In text parenthetical citations, such as those used by MLA and APA styles, direct the reader to the end of the report by using citation abbreviations, typically the author's last name, and the year of the publication. The full citation, in MLA or APA style, appears at the end of the report, in a Reference section that may be titled Works Cited or Bibliography. In research reports, citations may have provided information, even if they did not result in a complete citation. These would appear in the Bibliography as well. Entries in a Works Cited section appear at the end of the report and are listed in alphabetical order by the author's last name.

Another type of referencing involves placing footnotes in the document itself, at the bottom of the page where the citation reference is made. This is a convenient way for the reader to see the source of the citation without having to look at the end of the report, as with the Works Cited page. In terms of placement, the footnotes would be noted in the text with a footnote marker, and placed at the end of the document, in an Endnotes pages in the order in which they appeared.

The Problem-Solving Process We recall that the basis for writing a report is to solve a problem. Therefore, before proceeding to appropriate research methods, the problem statement needs to be defined as well as a statement of purpose for the report. The problem statement is the problem that needs to be solved by conducting the research and writing the report. The statement of purpose for the report is essentially the goal of the research. An example of this would be that an IT company needs to expand its visibility, and it has been relying on a minimal Website, word of mouth networking, and LinkedIn to build its customer base. The problem is that this company perceives an upcoming decline in business revenue, due to a major credit card company not using the IT company's outstanding superior services in the coming year. The statement of purpose for the report then is to assess current business for this company, as well as future goals regarding the level of desired expansion, expressed in number of clients, location of clients, needed revenue, and desired profit.

It is important to define the scope of the research before moving into the actual research phase of the report. The report must be of a workable size, with a budget and staff that fit the scope of the project. It is critical to know of any limitations before the research begins.

Research Methods   Primary and secondary research methods are used to collect data, and you can use either or both. Primary research is original and may need to be conducted if secondary, or already proven research methods, are not enough.

Primary research methods could include online surveys, in person or phone interviews, and observational methods that are then analyzed. There are benefits and perhaps disadvantages to conducting primary research. One of the advantages of conducting original research is that it may gather more current information than secondary research. In addition, whereas secondary research may give

FIGURE 17 *Market research terms.*

insight into a relevant topic, it may not meet all the requirements of the current project; therefore, building on the secondary research but focusing differently or adding new elements would provide benefits.

Disadvantages of instituting primary research could be cost, time, and not having the advantage of testing the research, as is the case with secondary research that has already been established. Nevertheless, there are times when either or both methods need to be employed. Primary research falls into three basic categories: surveys, direct observation, and experimentation.

Surveys The first aspect of developing a survey is to determine the target audience. Because you cannot always reach 100% of the population, you need to form what is termed a sample. A sample includes a representative number of recipients of the whole group.

There are two areas of caution when conducting a survey: controlling for bias in the sample and controlling for sampling error. Both of these errors can occur if the sampling is not representative enough of the group. Often if a particular segment of the sample is not accessible, or other mitigating factors arise during the research process, these are noted in the introduction of the report.

Other cautions relate to the validity and the reliability of the survey. A survey is valid if it measures what it is intended to measure and deals with the accuracy of the measurement. This can be achieved by wording questions carefully and making sure that the questions represent what you are asking. Validity can be further established by conducting a pilot test and then refining it before disseminating it more widely.

Reliability deals with the consistency of the measurement and the degree to which the questions elicit the same or similar data when used under the same conditions. It can be achieved by repeating the survey, and by making sure that enough of a sampling occurs so that certain patterns and trends can be noted. A sample of 20 may not be enough to establish results that may be seen with a larger sample of 100 or 200. The researcher needs to know that if the survey were given to a larger audience, the responses would not be significantly altered; in other words, that the survey was well constructed, and was given to a representative enough group of recipients. Surveys are often delivered online, so results can be received immediately and the data can be downloaded into databases and spreadsheets for easy organization and analysis. A few common online survey sites include www.SurveyMonkey™.com and www.SurveyGizmo.com, but an easy Google search will reveal hundreds more. Surveys can be conducted in hard copy format, with individuals penciling in the answers to the questions, but this is a tedious task and better suited to creation of online- or e-mail-based surveys. The

FIGURE 18 *Hard copy and electronic surveys.*

checkboxes you see in the image below could be converted to fillable boxes using common word processing or related software such as Adobe Acrobat Writer©. The results are then collected and placed in databases where the data can be easily manipulated and organized for final analysis.

Best Practices for Survey Design

A very comprehensive white paper on Best Practice for Survey Design can be found at Survey Monkey.com.

Direct Observation

Direct observation involves observing certain phenomena in their natural setting and then analyzing the results. It differs from an experimental setting where an artificial environment is created for control purposes and a variable is then introduced. With direct observation you want to see events exactly as they are occurring and take note of what is happening. It is different from taking notes on variables as you introduce them.

Observing with a purpose requires the same type of thorough preparation and quality control: agreement among all observers regarding the understanding of the purpose of the observations, consistency and clarity in questions asked, and attention to the environment and context. To make sure that businesses are checking for appropriate identification for persons buying alcohol, quality control through direct observation could consist of sending a team of representatives to various businesses in their region, on a rotating schedule, to observe, without identifying themselves, the behavior of the cashiers who are checking out customers with alcohol purchases. That behavior would then be noted, collected, and given to the home office, with decision making occurring as a result of the direct observation data.

Experimentation

In experimental research, one or more controlled samples is tested before a variable is then added and manipulated for part of the experiment. Then any differences in the two experiments are noted and analyzed. For example, a software company is introducing a new version of accounting software. A study could be conducted within the accounting department that involves creation of an in-house training program that allows employees to learn the software on their own time, in the morning before work, and during the lunch hour. The degree to which they learn the software within a given timeframe could be measured. A second experiment with a new variable could be conducted on the same employees. This time employees are required to attend a certain number of hours of training, whereas in the initial study attendance was voluntary. The same measurement of skill level acquired would be examined and the two studies could then be compared in light of the new variable.

Secondary Data The use of the computer has made sifting through numerous databases a much easier task. At www.infoplease.com, a 2008 survey shows that 89% of Internet users use a search engine to find data, followed by e-mail use, which was 92% at the time of the survey (Information Please Database, 2008).

Historically researchers used physical, not online, libraries, sorted through card indexes and catalogs and other sources, took handwritten notes on note cards, and sorted and filed them manually. They may have physically copied and pasted the results, with glue, to storyboards for a marketing presentation! They were not using the copy and paste features in word processing software.

Currently, to collect already gathered and proven, or secondary research, we typically use a search engine such as Google, or an industry related search engine such as DogPile®, which is a meta search engine—a search engine that searches other search engines and provides the best results from them. We use key words typed into a search box to conduct searches, regardless of the search engine chosen. Key words are identified by breaking down the sentence or concept, typically starting with the main subject or noun, then its adjectives and the elimination of introductory phrases or prepositions and articles.

To be truly effective in Internet searches, it is important to understand how the search engine performs the search. It is different from using a subject directory. Instead, a search engine uses programs called spiders to crawl the Web, logging the words on each page. The search engine scans its own very large database,

© Mikhail Nekrasov, 2012. Used under license from Shutterstock, Inc.

FIGURE 19 *Index cards—Old school!*

FIGURE 20 *Cut, Copy, and Paste functions with Word.*

and then returns hyperlinks to Websites that contain the key search words that the researcher typed in the search box.

Not all search engines support Boolean logic, but using Boolean's logical operands, such as AND, OR, IF, THEN, ELSE, to broaden or narrow your search refines the search immensely. "Boolean searching is built on a method of symbolic logic developed by George Boole, a 19th century English mathematician" according to Boswell, in an article discussing how to make Web searches more effective and sophisticated, thereby eliminating many unneeded documents in the results (Boswell 2012).

Collaborative Reports

Collaborative writing in general and collaborative report writing is a very popular, valued, and powerful business process. Businesses are comprised of groups—departments, and other organizational units that lend themselves to working in teams. Some of the most valuable skills that employers cite repeatedly include excellence in spoken and written communication skills, as well as the ability to work well in teams. This is the perfect triangulation of skills.

Group meetings where collaborative writing takes place can occur in a number of different formats. They can be held Face-to-Face (F2F), remotely using video conferencing technology such as Skype or GoToMeeting, or online in Webinars, which is the Web-based term for seminars.

The concept of a group-writing situation is somewhat daunting and maybe even confusing for someone who has not been involved intimately in that situation. But with roles clearly outlined and procedures managed well throughout the length of the project, there is more to be gained by putting many brains together in a synergistic fashion than by placing total responsibility upon one person.

Imagine that you are attending a department meeting. Your particular expertise has been noted because you have successfully written a $50,000 grant for company expansion into different markets, and your department received the money. The reward for good work and getting noticed is trust—trust in you accepting more responsibility and seeing it through to successful completion. Therefore, you are tasked with writing a variety of documents for the organization. They include: updating the "Policies and Procedures" manual for the company, developing a handout on "Conflict Resolution in Small Group Meetings," and writing a manual on "Best Practices for Writing White Papers." Clearly, you will need help with these writing tasks, even though you were the one individual given a certain degree of notoriety in the company for having written the grant proposal and receiving the funds. Clearly, you need help writing. Logically, you would start by creating a group for each one of the three written documents. Once the needed group members have been determined, strategies are carried out to proceed to the writing and editing phases.

Strategies for Group Writing

In a group-writing situation, you will need to decide who will be the project lead. Often, it is best to have one person with excellent and proven writing skills oversee the entire writing project, and divide the project into chunks. It could be chapters, sections of a manual, or groups of slides in a PowerPoint presentation. After delegating, set a timeline and send a group e-mail invitation to all members of the group, reminding them of the writing deadlines periodically and inviting them to the group meeting sessions as well.

After members have written the first draft, call a meeting where the entire group then reads and discusses the work of each individual. The written portions should be e-mailed as attachments in a user-friendly editable fashion, typically a current version of Word, before the meeting so that people have a chance to carefully review the document in advance, or it could be posted to a Wiki or to Google Docs, both tools where joint authoring, review, and editing can take place. If, however, you want the recipient of the document to just read and not have editing privileges, you can send it in a read only format, such as a PDF file.

FIGURE 21 *Group writing meeting.*

Make sure that the roles of "reader" and/or "reviewer" or "editor" are clear in the beginning stages of delegating the writing to members.

The revision process can be lengthy. It is important to give the group reasonable deadlines within which to accomplish the research, writing, and editing tasks. Revisions can occur collaboratively, in face-to-face meetings, or online via wikis and shared documents, and be overseen by the primary editor who is responsible for that portion of the writing.

Final considerations involve how the writing will ultimately be presented. There is always a purpose for a document to be written, as in the case of the three written documents we have been discussing. A Policies and Procedures Manual might be posted to a Website and sent as a PDF document attachment via company e-mail. Conflict Resolution in Small Group Meetings may result in a research report of medium-large scope and be published on the Internet as well as within the company Website. It may be used in orientation meetings for new employees, so it may be part of a hard copy printed document disseminated at a new employee orientation. Best Practices for Writing White Papers would be posted to the internal company Website, as well as to its external Website so that external clients and vendors could access it.

© Dmitriy Shironosov, 2012. Used under license from Shutterstock, Inc.

Finally, good collaborative writing is part of good communication. Today with the use of the Internet and other technologies, effective multi-person oral and written communication is occurring constantly. These technologies include real time or synchronous communications via portable devices like cell phones with integrated applications for chatting, texting, and video conferencing in real time. Meeting reminders, attachments sent via e-mail and accessed via a smart phone, and online conferences and presentations accessible via portable devices, such as laptops and smart phones, increase real time expediency and the capabilities of group writing and collaboration in general. Though these devices and technologies are available and greatly enhance the process of collaboration, at the very least a F2F meeting should be held in the beginning stages of the group writing process as well as when the final draft is approved. In these meetings, the written documents can be downloaded from a laptop or other computer, even a smart phone, which is connected to a Liquid Crystal Display (LCD) and projected to the group. The presenter can scroll through the various sections of the document and edit in real time. If it is not possible to be in the same physical location, a videoconference can be used for these critical startup and concluding meetings.

For group document review, there is a convenient tool called Track Changes in the Review Menu of Word that allows a color to be assigned to a particular reviewer so that edits can be easily tracked. The markups or edits in this feature can be turned on and off as needed.

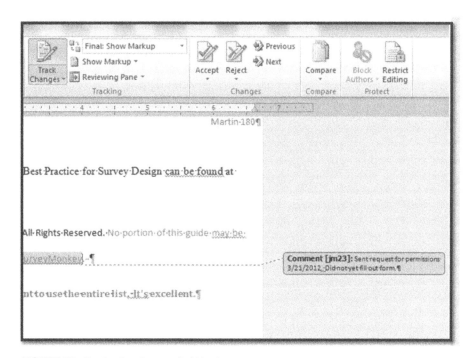

FIGURE 22 *Reviewing feature in Word.*

Student Activity Pages

 Choose a topic of interest in current, Business Communications. It could be a topic discussed in previous chapters of the textbook, or something that you are interested in.

Formulate the problem, use secondary research methodology to analyze the data you collect, and formulate a solution. Use Word Templates to format the report as a short report in a White Paper format, or format as a PowerPoint presentation Incorporate many of the organizational, graphic, and quantitative data elements discussed in this chapter, including a minimum of a table, a section with bullets, a section with indents, and a section with an outline. Also, include at least one Excel chart of your choosing to demonstrate a process or quantitative data.

Publish the White Paper or PowerPoint presentation to your blog site, and/or to your online classroom site, or as instructed.

■ **TEAMWORK**

Working in the groups created in Chapters 1 and 2, as assigned by your instructor, create the following documents and proposals. You will be writing a one page persuasive proposal, a 10 page white paper and a 10-slide PowerPoint presentation based on the proposal and the white paper. This is a team project. Working in groups as assigned by your instructor, create the following documents and proposals. Remember to use your favorite search engine to find "best practices" and "sample documents" for a one page "Persuasive Proposal" and a "ten page White Paper" and integrate these into a 10-slide PowerPoint presentation.

Prompt: You are looking for a company that will provide you with the best e-mail marketing campaign services. You need them to build your Website, manage your database of prospective clients, track the results of the e-mails, and provide analytics. Use the White Paper in Figure 5.13 as a guide to the services this company must provide. After searching, decide as a group which company to pitch to your company's executive team. Then create the Persuasive Request, White Paper, and PowerPoint presentation based on what you have found.

Rely on the strengths of each of the members in your group to create these winning documents. Share the work accordingly.

Use Word for the Persuasive Request and the White Paper. Make use of the Themes in the Page Layout Tab menu in Word to apply template styles that rival those best practices you see in Figures 5.12 & 5.13 and online in your searches. Include an automated cover page, a table of contents, page numbers, headers and/ or footers, and a works cited.

Use PowerPoint for the PowerPoint presentation.

Create three links to the three documents on your blog site. They can be in PDF format or any other format that you prefer.

Study the sample white paper in the textbook, and the white paper template in the Chapter Six link on your grtep.com Website. Also, google "sample white papers"n the Internet.

http://buscommwithanedge.wordpress.com/ is
marked private by its owner. If you were invited to
view this site, please **log in** below. Read more about
privacy settings.

Username

Password

☐ Remember Me   Log In

Register | Lost your password?

FIGURE 17 *Your classroom WordPress site.*

10 points each – 50 total	Persuasive Request	White Paper	PowerPoint Presentation
Content			
Layout & Design			
Grammar, Spelling & Writing Style			
Teamwork			
Technical Prowess			

Grading Rubric

Chapter Five

Communicating Orally

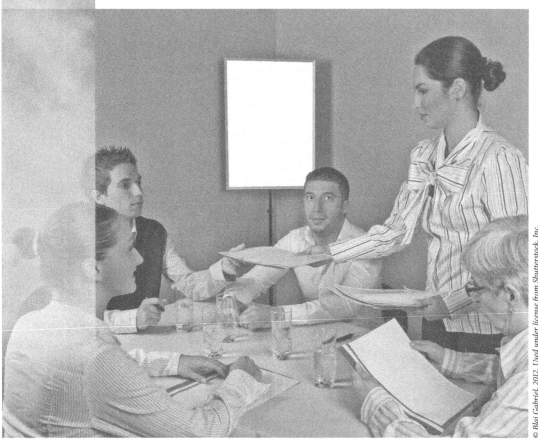

Chapter Six

Learning Objectives

LO1 Identify consequences of failed interpersonal communication.

LO2 Identify effective communication on the phone and in meetings.

LO3 Describe effective leadership techniques in meetings.

LO4 Demonstrate effective oral presentation skills.

When Interpersonal Communication Fails

There are many angles that this author could have used to approach this topic. A valid question to introduce the chapter might be "what percentage of your time is spent communicating orally on the job?" Common sense, and reflecting on some of our own work experiences, lead us to an answer that would most likely indicate that we communicate verbally on the job a good part of the day. We can categorize and quantify the types of communication, the time spent on that communication, and how important we perceive that communication to be to us personally and to the organization. These are all logical considerations for a discussion on forms of oral communication.

However, perhaps a more important question to ask ourselves is what are the consequences of our daily frequent communications when they fail, or are not as effective as they should be? One of the primary purposes of this text is to teach you how to communicate more effectively both in writing and orally. We communicate to convey information for a particular purpose. So we need to consider what happens when that good communication fails that we strive to achieve. What are the consequences of failed communication on the part of the sender, the receiver, or both? In realizing the dire consequences of failed communication, we can embrace with sincerity the need to constantly improve our communication and listening skills.

We can start with a compelling and famous example of the space shuttle *Challenger* that broke into pieces as the world watched on January 28, 1986, with seven American astronauts on board. How could some of the finest brains in the country have been responsible for this tragedy, many asked? Though the O-rings, which malfunctioned under a certain temperature, were found to have been the problem, what was more disconcerting was the finding that Thiokol engineers knew of the problem the night before the launch. They feared that the O-rings might fail under these conditions, and raised those fears vehemently to their superiors that night with raised voices and pounding fists. But the Thiokol engineers were overruled by NASA. The flight proceeded as scheduled, and at 11:38 AM, the shuttle broke apart 73 seconds into the flight, killing all seven crewmembers on board (Berkes, 2006). This is clearly a worst-case scenario of failed communications, but a very real and public case, with highly skilled, intelligent, and respected players.

So how did communication fail? Engineers expressed expert opinions with an appropriate degree of emotion. The management team at NASA, who were the appropriate recipients, received the communications. Nevertheless, the engineers' communications were ineffective. The recipients were not listening to the experts. They were listening instead to their own mandates to proceed with the launch. Their own internal perception that they must launch, in the face of much public scrutiny, was a stronger message than that of the experts who knew whether it was safe to launch.

 Student Activity 7.1.

- In addition to the O-Ring failure, how did the hierarchical chain of command affect what happened with the *Challenger* disaster? Research in a two-page paper what happened 17 years later with the explosion of the space shuttle Columbia. Approach it from the standpoint of whether you think that NASA fixed the problems with internal communications in the 17-year period between the two disasters. Use citations and follow the format of a short report in MLA format.

Sending Your Message Across the Divide— Communicating with an Edge

What does the "Sending Your Message Across the Divide-communicating with an Edge" subtitle mean to you? Metaphorically speaking, we can perceive any degree of distance, whether it be physical or psychological, hierarchical rank or perceived agendas, as a "divide" or a challenge to overcome. If we know entering into the communication process that we may be faced with any of the above challenges on the receiving end of that process, then perhaps we will work harder to send a very effective message and to follow up on the response to that message, until it is absolutely certain, in critical cases, that the message is received and internalized such that action will follow the receipt of the message. To ascertain whether our message has been received according to its intent, then we will engage with more sincerity and focus in active listening.

One third of employers replied to a ManpowerGroup survey that they cannot fill jobs because they cannot find enough qualified candidates (Groth, 2011). Of the employers polled, 17% said that the lack of "soft" skills or interpersonal and communication skills accounted for that difficulty, among other factors. Because we develop interpersonal skills over time, due to environment and upbringing, educators and managers feel that it is challenging to find ways to change those behavioral patterns. However, learning to improve interpersonal and communication skills is an achievable goal. Generally speaking, for both sender and receiver, concentration and focus will improve both speaking and listening skills.

FIGURE 1 *Communicating across the divide—OR making it across the communication chasm*

The Importance of Phone Skills   Often the first communication that occurs with a client is a phone conversation. It is important that this first impression is positive. A good first impression involves several factors. Tone of voice, content, and listening skills are all essential elements of proper phone etiquette.

You can practice "smiling" over the phone by leaving a mirror next to your workstation. Check your facial expressions. Those facial expressions will come across in your tone of voice and even the words you choose to express yourself with the client. Make sure that you are representing the company in a positive fashion consistently.

Regarding the tone of your voice and the tone of the message, start with a formal tone, and only move to a more informal tone if the relationship is one that is established and trusted. Often there will be a script that an organization will provide regarding what information to convey in various phone calls at different levels of servicing the customer. Even if a client becomes impatient or is dissatisfied with the service at some level, it is important for you to lead the conversation in a positive direction. The old adage "the customer is always right" should not be interpreted in a completely literal fashion, because the customer is not always right, and actually often is not right. However, the adage is a reminder that it is your customer; it is all right if the person is wrong; and, most importantly, you need to listen to the customer and eventually move to the point where there is mutual understanding and agreement on what needs to occur next. The guest is always the guest and the customer always the customer—you hope. You are the one offering the service, conveying your organization's message to the public, and it is important that you remain as positive, calm, and reassuring as possible, even in the midst of your clients' frustrations, when they will inevitably occur.

It is important to reach a balance in the phone conversation between conveying essential information and listening carefully to the client. Active listening involves taking steps to remain actively involved in the conversation for purposes of information gathering for follow-up. Taking notes is an effective way to stay engaged and to gather information. While speaking, you may be taking notes for an e-mail follow-up or inputting to an electronic calendaring program that contains a client note section under the contact profile information.

Finally, if you need to leave a message for a client, or take a message from a client, it is important to include the necessary details in the message. Time, date, reason for the call, and contact information, such as a phone number or an e-mail address, are common pieces of information. More complex communications in larger organizations with a dedicated customer service department will allow the servicer to access database levels that allow the person to input financial and account data. Often the service that is provided by larger companies, such as credit card, mortgage, and insurance companies, will have a first responder level of customer service that allows phone representatives to access only certain areas of the database; therefore, the servicer can only provide the client with a certain level of servicing before needing to transfer to a supervisor. This segmentation in servicing is often frustrating for the customer, as he will need to be placed on hold again, repeat his personal information again for database accuracy purposes, and then have to essentially repeat the history of the conversation that he just completed with the previous representative. It is increasingly more important due to this type of segmentation that the customer service representative be an effective listener and provide support and understanding to the customer who is "always right"!

Communicating Effectively in Meetings Participating effectively in a meeting is an important oral communication skill. We used the example of the *Challenger* Space Shuttle disaster previously in this chapter to highlight the importance of communication skills, using a worst-case scenario of what happens when communication fails. This example was a visible example of failure, from the TV coverage of the disaster that many millions of viewers saw occurring in the Florida sky that fateful morning, to the visible O-Ring failures; however, the less tangible, but very real failure that occurred dealt with failed communication. In this same way, a palpable yet rather insidious communication pattern can be occurring as an undercurrent in an organization, which is not visible until some other more visible failure occurs, or the company steadily loses revenue for a few months or even years. Only then do the problems come into focus.

The definition of the word insidious at http://dictionary.reference.com reveals the word as a behavior that can occur at several different levels from "intended to entrap or beguile" to "stealthily treacherous or deceitful" to "proceeding in an inconspicuous or seemingly harmless way but actually with grave effect" (http://dictionary.reference.com n.d., retrieved 2012). Usually this latter case occurs inside organizations. This type of behavior is difficult to track and manage, until some more overt sign or result shows itself from an insidious proceeding(s) that is seemingly harmless but actually has a grave effect. We can all think of communications that do not surface until there is such discord among parties that it is difficult to resolve.

So how do we avoid having communication digress to this level? There are actually techniques of conducting oneself in a meeting, as well as conducting the meeting. Let us examine the first scenario, related to participating effectively in a meeting. Techniques include listening carefully, coming prepared with appropriate information and facts, planning the message before you speak, giving other people a turn, and following the agenda. If you are in a meeting that is well conducted, it is easy to participate in the above stated fashion. Cues to alert you that you are talking too much or not on task include being redirected by the meeting leader or by your peers. Feeling inappropriately informed or prepared is another signal that you should come to the next meeting with more information. Finally, if you feel frustrated at any level with how a meeting is progressing, speak to a colleague, a peer, or even the meeting leaders themselves regarding how you feel. It can avoid miscommunication later. Take the time, however, to think about your approach first. Make it positive and have a particular positive outcome in mind that will serve both you and the organization well. It is important to weigh the consequences of not speaking up about a particular issue with the consequences of speaking up. It is more common for employees to be silent about issues over which they have concerns, than to speak up, due to perceived consequences of being labeled negatively and of damaging valued relationships, especially with those above them in the organizational chain of command (Milliken, 2003).

Leading Effectively in Meetings   In some cultures, social status and rank determine who speaks up, when, and to whom. However, when chairing a democratically based meeting, it is important to hear both the majority and the minority voice. Given the research cited in the previous paragraph, how do you elicit valuable feedback and dialogue from your valued employees, each one with their own unique contributions? These voices add to the success of an organizational unit, and ultimately to the success of the organization as a whole. Fortunately, there are techniques to employ to be successful as a meeting leader as well as a meeting participant. There are many online

© Monkey Business Images, 2012. Used under license from Shutterstock, Inc.

FIGURE 2 *Natural leaders capture the attention of the group.*

sources, textbooks, and business practices to reference that will assist you in this leadership role.

One such reference is the popular *Robert's Rules of Parliamentary Procedures.* Commonly referred to as Robert's Rules of Order, the text was originally written to help private organizations conduct business, but many legislative bodies and other organizations and businesses have adopted the rules. The book was written in 1876 by Henry Martyn Robert, an Army engineer, to help him manage a raucous church meeting. The book is 300 pages long!

Plan the Meeting and Create An Agenda

If you are a meeting leader, the first step in conducting a good meeting is careful planning. An agenda should be planned and written and should be disseminated before the meeting, so that participants can see if they are on the agenda and plan accordingly. Items should be listed in logical order or order of importance, and action items should remain on the agenda until they have been resolved.

Follow The Agenda

The person chairing the meeting should be leading the participants by following the agenda and moving the meeting along to the next agenda item, after sufficient dialogue occurs. It is typical not to resolve all agenda items in the course of one meeting, so those items remain on the next agenda. Action items should always follow through to the next agenda until they are successfully resolved.

Participation

An effective facilitator encourages participation from all members in the group. As we discussed previously, acknowledge and include all participants who each contribute unique input for the team. The group leader can call on individuals who might not otherwise speak up, especially if the perception is that their opinion might be an unpopular minority opinion.

Patterson, et al., in their popular text *Crucial Confrontations,* writes about the benefits of confronting others and the costs of walking away, and discusses how accountability and morale are improved by learning "crucial confrontation techniques" (Patterson, pp. 14–15).

Controlling the Meeting

In any group meeting, certain people tend to talk too much and dominate the dialogue. Alliances form within an organization and friends will chat with friends and encourage one another. In addition, personality type and perceived rank in the company will determine who speaks up, how quickly, and how often. To accommodate all members of the group given these considerations, it is necessary for the facilitator to control the amount of time that members speak, and to encourage discussion from those who are silent. It may even sometimes be necessary to institute specific time limits, especially when there is much debate. Assigning a timekeeper to keep this process in check is a valuable technique.

Oral Communication with Formal Presentations

Oral presentations can be dynamic, visual, and convincing. They allow for the addition of the spoken voice and visualizations in a way that cannot be achieved in written reports. They also create an environment of spontaneity and a very real time exchange of information, as well as the ability to check for understanding or influence. Therefore, they are highly valued in an organization. In fact, those who are successful at giving formal presentations often receive more benefits from a company than those who are not.

However, oral presentations are often a forum that many individuals fear. Much research lists the fear of public speaking as one of the highest ranked fears in common surveys. Many Best Practices sites and lists as well as tips and techniques can be instituted to help the presenter give a dynamic and effective speech.

© Everett Collection, 2012. Used under license from Shutterstock, Inc.

FIGURE 3 *"That was then." Oratory skills and writing skills were highly refined because that was the only medium for communication. Absent were technology and diversity.*

FIGURE 4 *"This is Now!" Present are technology and diversity.*

One of the first factors to consider when preparing an oral presentation is how the audience will listen, and for how long. It is critical to realize that the audience will be able to listen to the first ten minutes or so in a very focused fashion but that the attention will wane. People are easily distracted. Therefore, the presenter needs to alter the approach. Tone of voice can be raised and lowered—as both of these techniques catch attention; visual displays can be introduced and changed, and audience participation may be encouraged. Breaks at natural topic changes are effective. A question and answer period with little rewards for the "winner" directly engages the audience. In classrooms and meetings, Web and classroom clickers are given to the attendees to "vote" on questions, issues, or surveys in an anonymous fashion.

If we were to institute a ten-step process for giving formal, oral presentations, they would include the following:

1. *Know the audience*

   A highly underrated aspect of presenting is knowing the audience. This includes knowing their educational level, technical level of expertise, and cultural differences, which are present in today's global economy. The information about the audience should be acquired before any planning of the presentation takes place. Question colleagues or team members to discover the interests and hobbies of your attendees. The more common ground you can establish before the presentation, the more open the audience will be to internalizing the information you present.

2. *Capture the message of the presentation in one single sentence.*

Start with it. End with it. Create emphasis. Emphasize the main points of the presentation and return to them often, in different formats, stated differently, or visualized in several different types of charts and graphs.

3. *Present the information in a logical or chronological, or audience interest-based fashion.*

Chronological order is not always the best way to present data. Portions of data, such as time and date sensitive charts or progressions, need to be shown in this fashion; however, data can be presented in an order that might appeal to audience interest, as assessed in the first step of the process.

4. *Strive to create a strong introduction and an equally strong conclusion.*

Capture your audience when audience focus is at its peak in the beginning of the presentation. This is achieved by presenting a clear and concise message, using a strong voice, introducing music or a joke, or a story, or a visual message. Show the audience the order of the content in the presentation as you would in a formal report. Create the all-important introductory paragraph.

5. *Use visualizations effectively.*

We cannot avoid using the adage "A picture is worth a thousand words." It is. Perhaps it is worth much more than a thousand words. It conveys a rich, complex message seen through an amazing instrument—the eyes. Visualizations should be used to support information, to enhance information, and to show data and trends.

6. *Timing—practice and perfect it!*

Timing is everything—another very important adage. Timing is a skill that is learned from giving many presentations. You read the audience, choose your starting point, and command attention by moving through the information. Introduce more emphasis by raising the volume of your voice or by increasing the speed of the presentation when you see focus drifting—or by slowing down when it seems that the audience needs further clarification or understanding. There is much satisfaction in giving a presentation that you know is well timed, because your audience will show that they understand by their attention to you during the presentation and by the praises lauded on you after the presentation.

7. *Know the technology you are using. Choose it appropriately.*

Digital display presenters, Liquid Crystal Displays (LCDs), white boards, overhead projectors, and software such as PowerPoint, or examples from the Internet are some of the many current forms of technology. Know your technology well before presenting and arrive early to make sure everything is working. Practice running through the presentation in the seminar or workplace room before the audience arrives. This also helps to calm the natural nervousness that many feel before giving a presentation.

Use digital display presenters to show a variety of objects to the audience, from paper maps to artifacts. White boards with touch screen capability and Smart Boards are interactive tools that allow the presenter to work comfortably, to speak, and to move back and forth between the screen and the computer with ease. Overhead projectors are still used in some arenas, but the Document Display presenters are becoming more common. PowerPoint deserves attention as a very powerful multimedia tool that can incorporate narrated sound, background music, and video, as well as professionally formatted text boxes and graphics, such as line and bar charts and graphs. The presentation can be saved in various formats for sending via e-mail as a PowerPoint show, or saved as an HTML file for Web posting and viewing.

8. *Communicate, and perform.*

Communication is a two way process. Communicate with your audience. Engage them. Ask questions. Write the answers on the board. Give a mini quiz halfway through the presentation. Take a break and then share the results of the quiz to be graded by the individuals themselves, to keep it "safe." Read your audience during the presentation to make sure that they are following you. Make sure their eyes are on you, the "show." There is an element of acting involved in presenting. However, do not get so lost in your own performance that you forget to ask questions of the audience or to involve them in the process of the presentation by providing them with some interactions to engage them.

9. *Control the nerves, but direct the nervous energy to get you* through it.

Nerves are not necessarily a bad thing. Nerves stimulate the senses. You can learn how to capture this energy and use it to your advantage. Practicing is the best way to manage your nerves and showing up early for the presentation helps as well.

10. *Stimulate the senses.*

Increasingly we are living in a multimedia world where sound and sight are stimulated wherever we go. Presentation software is an excellent program that supports many different forms of multimedia, and your audience will expect or at least appreciate the inclusion of sensory media. For example, if you are giving a marketing PowerPoint presentation on a particular product, like saffron, Figure 7.1, you might want to bring a small piece of the beautiful herb to the presentation and allow the audience to pass it around and touch it, smell it, and comment on it. Pause the presentation to give them the chance to do this.

Add a soothing background sound with music from Persia and a map of the regions where saffron is grown and show people cultivating it in the fields. Give

© Subbotina Anna, 2012. Used under license from Shutterstock, Inc.

FIGURE 5 *Saffron.*

some history of the product before moving into the selling stage of the presentation, where we are accustomed to seeing charts and graphs and where we sometimes repel the information if it is presented in too dry a fashion. All of this creates a very soft smooth entry to allow the audience to transition into a sensory place, which makes the presentation of the numbers, and more expected information, more palpable and acceptable. If the mind is a relaxed and accepting place, the audience is more likely to focus on and internalize all the data in the presentation.

PowerPoint Presentation Tips and Techniques

- Choose an appropriate theme from those in the program. Do not change it too much. Layout artists and graphic designers designed the themes. Trust them to know design and color.

- Research and write the content of the presentation, then trim it down so that you do not have too much content.

- Do not include more than five lines of text per slide.

- Use at least a 48-point font so that the audience can see from a distance.

- Show main points with charts and graphs. Customize one of the bars on a chart with the company logo or some other meaningful icon.

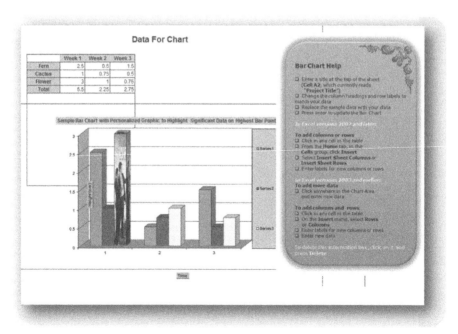

FIGURE 6 *Sample bar chart with personalized graphic.*

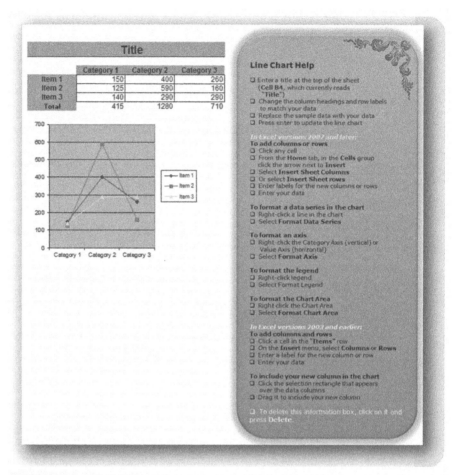

FIGURE 7 *Sample line chart.*

■ Use a music video to create interest.

■ Imbed a YouTube video link and click on it to show the video directly from YouTube.

Insert a background sound clip for the first slide or two, and run it continuously while the room is filling.

■ Have your handouts, props, or promotional materials laid out on a table so that attendees can peruse them as they enter, while the introductory slides and music are playing.

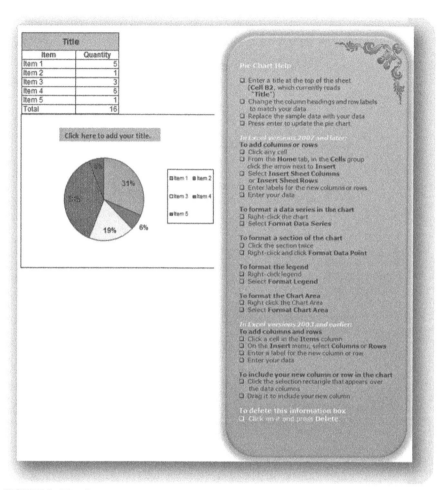

FIGURE 8 *Pie chart.*

- Advance to the next slide, after making your strong introductory statements.

- Consider using narration on certain slides. It adds auditory interest. People will want to hear your voice recorded, as well as your "in person" voice.

- Include hyperlinks, but test them to make sure they still work before presenting.

- Include customized bullets and backgrounds with the company logo or another significant logo or icon that means something to the audience.

- Insert the three graphs here from the sample templates from Excel.

- Create a dramatic beginning and ending that introduce your subject in one sentence. Include that sentence in your ending and add any other conclusions as appropriate.

- End with a slide or two with music and graphics. Then turn on the lights and bring your audience back to the present!

There are, however, skeptics who believe that the use of presentation software such as PowerPoint actually dummies down data, oversimplifying ideas that should be presented in a more complex fashion. In his essay "The Cognitive Style of PowerPoint" Edward Tufte (Tufte, 2006, 2nd ed.), the author, states that "In 28 books on PP presentations, the 217 data graphics depict an average of 12 numbers each."

In fact, the Columbia Accident Investigation Board at NASA cited PowerPoint as a culprit in the Columbia space shuttle crash of 2003, due to a confusing PowerPoint slide "crammed with nested bullet points and irregular short forms" (Thomson, 2003). However, Thomson goes on to state that Microsoft officials differ with this opinion, essentially claiming that using PowerPoint is a matter of choice, that many prefer simplifying data, and that Tufte prefers dense information, rather than simple data. He concludes his articles by stating that Colin Powell chose PowerPoint to show the United Nations that Iraq possessed weapons of mass destruction. Clearly, there are choices regarding if and how to use PowerPoint as a presentation tool. Data visualization merits careful consideration.

Communication in the Workplace Categorized At North Carolina State University, an interesting study was conducted on communication behavior in the workplace (Covington), using performance-based questions.

As this study suggests, we need to emphasize effective oral communication, as well as the need to collaborate for longer projects and documents, because of the high percentage of time professionals spend performing these activities on the job.

Appendix D
Statistical Analysis

Factor Analysis

Five survey questions involve similar variable related to professionals' communication behavior (see Appendix A, questions 11, 12, 13, 14, and 15). These performance-based questions lend themselves to a factor analysis to construct summary scores for correlated activities. The rotated factor pattern revealed the following four factors with high loadings:

Factor 1	Time spent writing on the job	.80
	Writing in collaboration with others	.77
	Writing long, formal documents (e.g., reports, proposals)	.58
Factor 2	Oral communication on the phone	.75
	Group meetings via teleconference	.68
	Email	.58
Factor 3	Memos	.76
	Letters	.74
Factor 4	Chat online	.80
	International communication	.77

These factors show that technology has impacted how professionals communicate on the job. Factor 2 shows that those who communicate using the phone one-on-one also tend to use teleconferences and emails more frequently. More importantly, those who use chat also communicate more internationally.

Factor 1 shows that formal, long documents are created on the job in collaboration with others. Short, hard copy documents, such as memos and letters, are related activities as shown by Factor 3.

This suggests that as we teach professional communication to students, we need to emphasize collaborative work for longer documents, and we need to also focus on effective oral communication and email. Chat should be highlighted as we teach global communication techniques.

FIGURE 9 *Appendix D, Communication study, North Carolina State University.*

Student Activity Pages

■ TEAMWORK for ORAL PRESENTATIONS

Using the Persuasive Request, White Paper, and PowerPoint presentation created in Activity 6.1 in Chapter 6, break into your classroom groups and prepare to present the PowerPoint presentation that incorporates the Persuasive Request and the White Paper. No additional documents need to be prepared; however, you must practice presenting the presentation convincingly as a group. You may want to augment your PowerPoint presentation using some of the multimedia elements, such as sound, narration, videos, notes for the audience, and props, as discussed in the Tips and Techniques for PowerPoint in this chapter.

Rely on the strengths of each of the members in your group to involve everyone and present effectively. Share the work equally. Save as a PPT file and as a PPTS (a PowerPoint show) format. Present orally as a group and if you have an online class, upload to your online site, and post to your WordPress blog.

Job Search, The E-Portfolio: "Branding" Yourself

Chapter Seven

Learning Objectives

LO1 Build a current industry standard resume.

LO2 Learn to prepare an innovative portfolio package.

LO3 Engage in the job search process by using the prepared portfolio.

LO4 Follow up on resume material submittals.

There are many qualified college graduates and experienced job seekers who are looking for employment, but do they really know what types of materials industry is expecting them to submit? Often ill prepared and ineffective job application materials themselves are the only roadblocks to engaging in a job search process that nets results in the form of interviews and job offers. We want to assure that this very fixable roadblock is not keeping you from getting the job you desire, have prepared for, and deserve!

The Resume, First Impressions DO Count!

Current Industry Standard Resumes It is imperative that you remember that your beautiful smiling face, your glowing personality, your best dress or suit, or your handshake are NOT the first things a potential employer learns about you.

The first impression that the employer will see will come in the form of an electronic copy of your resume and e-mail cover letter. That's it! First impressions do count and this first impression has to be beautifully crafted.

In this part of the chapter, we will focus on how to craft a rather technical piece of writing—the resume. There is an industry expectation regarding the format and content of the resume that job seekers must understand and adhere to, if they wish to have employers consider their resume in a serious fashion. In addition, because employers sometimes receive hundreds of applications for just one job opening, the amount of time they can spend reading each resume or job application is very little. Remillard, an executive job recruiter, discusses how he can review a resume in 20 seconds or less, and states that the average time that he has spent reviewing resumes is 5 to 7 seconds (Remillard, 2010). However, once the resume has passed a certain set of initial criteria, then it gets a much more detailed analysis. Let us discuss how to make your resume pass that all-important first review.

Current Resume Writing Practice— Where To Find It

The best place to find current practices for resume and cover letter writing is from recruiters and job placement agencies in your area and on the Internet. These preferred standards change, so each time you seek a job, you must consult these references. Some of the larger companies, such as Accountemps, http://www.accountemps.com, in San Diego, will come to classrooms and speak, so finding a community college or library that offers job search classes and workshops is an excellent resource. These resources are effective because recruiters are the middle agent between job seekers and employers, so they can impartially interview and screen both parties. They also talk to hundreds of employers a year, so they really have the true pulse of the local job market. Often, employers' expectations regarding the format and substance of the resume are delivered to applicants and classrooms via recruiters.

Because writing a resume often seems to be an overwhelming process for most people, and because each part of the resume does have its own standards and key points, we will consider each part of the resume in depth, "building" it as we read, section by section.

Personal Information

Your name, address, phone, e-mail address, and a LinkedIn address are expected pieces of personal information. Some prefer not to include their home address, and this is fine as long as an e-mail address at the very minimum and a LinkedIn

FIGURE 1 *Accountemps® Job Placement and Recruiting Agency.*

address as a preferred piece of information are included. Your LinkedIn address will be under your Public Profile, once you are logged in.

Jackie Martin | 1234 White Horse Lane | Pleasantville, IN 09876
555-555-1212 | jmartin@abc.com | jmartin@LinkedIn

The Importance of the Summary Statement or Summary of Qualifications

We are living in a time where the practice in both business and non-profit organizations is to quantify data, to show or to prove a record of accomplishment. The Summary Statement, like the first sentence in a paragraph, is where this occurs. It is the first piece of the resume that an employer reads. The Summary Statement has replaced the "Job Objective," though you will still see Job Objective as the beginning piece for some resume examples. In the older resume format, the Job Objective read like this:

OLD

The old resume writing style uses "Job Objective," is passive, and asks for the job.

"Seeking a job with a company that will allow me to utilize my skills and experience."

That kind of statement really does not say much at all about the job seeker. Further, it is a model that "seeks" or "asks" for the job.

BETTER

A "proficient" summary statement is what a job search counselor or employer will typically see in resumes. It is not wrong, it is just not as effective and quantifiable as the employer expects. The steps involved in the following example are excellent steps to take to formulate the summary statement. Still, this example is not quite the current and best practice industry standard, if it is missing quantifiable data. Often, however, this is just the type of introduction that a job seeker writes—and an employer sees first. And, often, this type of opening does not create enough interest to read further.

If you were to write a resume for an Accounting Manager, the Summary Statement for this position would include several essentials parts: 1) a description of your "professional self," 2) your computer skills, 3) industry specific work and education or training and, finally, 4) transferable or soft skills.

You would write the Summary Statement in a "fragment sentence" fashion. In other words, when Spellchecker highlights this phrase as a fragment you do not need to correct it. For example, start with the phrase "Motivated creative accounting manager;" then add the computer skills "highly computer literate;", then industry specific experience, "experience in management, bookkeeping, A/R A/P;" then transferable skills, "punctual, dependable, team player; detail-oriented." Separate the phrases with semicolons. Now, putting these essential four parts together it reads:

The New Proficient Summary Statement

"Motivated creative accounting manager;" "highly computer literate;" "experienced in management, bookkeeping, A/R A/P;" "punctual, dependable, team player; detail-oriented."

Again, this example is common and not bad, but not as engaging, effective, and quantifiable as it should be to capture the recruiter or employer in 5 to 7 seconds! So, let us add some quantifiable data to show performance in this next example.

BEST

The cutting edge, industry standard resume begins with a strong summary of your skills and experience, quantified. Instead of asking for the job, you summarize boldly and succinctly in three or four lines your professional title, education, and experience, highlighting to the employer what you have to "offer"—a very different approach than asking for the job. Additionally, the Summary Statement quickly brands you to the employer, creating a first impression from a written piece of material.

The Summary Statement needs to be clear, well written, and engaging and include measurable accomplishments. It should answer "how many," "how much," or "for how long." If the summary statement engages the employer, he or she will read further.

Following are examples of Summary Statements for a Chief Executive Officer (CEO), a Project Manager, and an Administrative Professional:

CEO

Results-oriented Executive Manager offering more than 15 years of progressively increasing controller and financial management expertise. Proven ability to turn around struggling companies managing budgets of $500K— $20 million to build a positive income stream, by reducing costs by 10–20 % and improving efficiency of operations and personnel. Innovative, with a proven ability to foresee new market opportunities in the U.S. and abroad. Advanced computer skills; superior team building; and strong management capabilities.

Project Manager

Information Technology Project Manager with 20+ years' experience successfully managing technical teams of 10–50 and budgets of $1-$25 million for U.S. and International clients.

In this case, one sentence is sufficient because it includes quantified technical and management success, because computer skills are implied in the IT field, and because team management is the included soft skill.

Administrative Assistant

Executive Administrative Assistant with 10 years' experience providing administrative support to management teams of 5–15; in small to medium size corporations; highly skilled with the MS Office Suite; formatting, note taking and report writing; excellent meeting facilitation.

In this example, the writer states the number of years, the number of managers supported, the size of the company, and specific software and admin skills.

Note that the sentences are actually not complete sentences—but rather fragments. This is the style of writing used in a resume, as it is a brief of your skills and experience.

The adjectives used are strong and descriptive. Also notice that the CEO's professional title and responsibilities are mentioned first, then followed by the inclusion of computer skills, and, finally, but always, "soft skills." Though the technical aspect of any job is highly important, equally important are computer skills, which are a basic and required skill set, and soft skills, or the ability to communicate in writing and orally, as well as the ability to get along well with coworkers.

Remember, if the Summary of Qualifications statement is well written, this section will interest the reader to move on to the next section of the resume, the SKILLS or EDUCATION section, depending on the job applicant's emphasis.

■ Mid-chapter Students Activity 8.1

Use the Resume Templates in Word to review sample Summary Statements and Profiles. Go to Word, open a New Blank Document, and go to the Office Button (or File in 2003), New. The New command takes you to all templates. In the keyword search box, type the keywords "functional resume." Study the examples and try to model your Summary Statement for your own personal ideal job, after these examples as well as the examples in this text.

Skills Educate yourself regarding job skills required by employers as found in job postings, before writing the resume. In this way, you can tailor your skills and experience on your resume to meet those skills listed in the job ads. There is a particular industry jargon for job categories and skills. By reading the job ads online, you can educate yourself, and then have the proper terminology swimming in your head before starting the writing process.

The jobs section of "Craigslist.org" has become a dynamic and "advertising free" conduit between employee and employer. It operates in the United States, Canada, Europe, Asia, the Pacific and Middle East, Oceania, Latin America, and Africa. Though this .org site exists in worldwide locations, it is an excellent forum for the local job market for many small to medium size companies.

Zero in on your city by simply clicking on your city link. Not only can you specify the city, but also specific towns and cities within a large metropolis. The layout is simple, "grass roots," and very reflective of real jobs that employers need to have filled immediately. Next enter a search term. You must know what you are looking for and what you want to do, and know some industry language related to the job.

In a Staff Accountant position, for example, you may find some of the following industry jargon for job skills.

Staff Accountant

- Manage accounting operations

- Day-to-day finance

- General Journal Entries

- Manage cash flow

- Publish cash position statements

- Reconcile all major accounts to database

- Prepare monthly financial statements

- Prepare quarterly variance analysis reports

- Prepare annual budget

- Prepare management reports

- Assist with 401 K Plan administration

Notice that the items are bulleted and rather abbreviated and that these job skills are clearly related to accounting management.

Consider some of the language involved with a paralegal job. It will be administrative in nature.

Paralegal

- Intellectual Property Law experience

- Knowledgeable in Agreements and Contracts

- Immigration—Visa Petitions, Requirements

- Paralegal Certificate

- 2+ Years Paralegal experience

- Proficient in Microsoft Office

- Excellent Organizational skills

The best executive is the one who has sense enough to pick good men to do what he wants done, and the self-restraint to keep from meddling with them while they do it.

        —Theodore Roosevelt, 26th American President

CEO

- Proven Leadership through Effective Communication

- Group Facilitation

- Influence through Example

- Management

- Problem Identification and Applied Problem Solving

- Technical Expertise

- Specific Hardware and Software Expertise

- Specialized Skills in . . .

- Strategy and Tactics

- Executive Decision Making

- Organizational Effectiveness

Workforce Partnerships and Occupational Outlook Forecasts are also excellent Websites to find language associated with a particular job as well as complete job data. www.SanDiegoAtWork.com is one such source. These sites include job descriptions and salary ranges, forecast the job market by occupation, and provide future trends. This is critically important when planning to pursue an education in a particular degree that may not show job growth by the time you graduate.

Not only are these excellent places to learn how to write according to the job you are seeking, but this will also educate you regarding what skills the employer(s) is seeking in a particular job, and how much that employer is willing to pay. This research is extremely valuable and current.

So, from these sample sites, we can see that job skills are bulleted and written in phrases that reflect a particular job skill, and that the phrases reflect current industry jargon. This is a quick way for an employer to see the skill sets you possess—to receive a quick picture of your abilities. Not only do the job ads help with wording of your job skills, they will also be a critical component in writing the effective e-mail cover letter.

■ Mid-chapter Student Activity 8.2

Go to Craigslist.org and search job ads based on a job title or area that you are interested in or for which you feel qualified.

Download three or four ads, highlight the skills listed, and keep these. You will need them as a reference when completing the body of the e-mail message that has your resume attached.

Study the ads, many of them, in depth. Compare the qualifications employers are seeking, the pay, the duties, and the language used to describe the job skills.

Create a list of job skills that you possess based on your talent, and upon the experience and phrasing that you have found in the ads. Use proper industry jargon for the job skills that you possess.

Print them as well and keep in a folder. We will use the skills you identified to build the e-mail "cover letter." Highlighting the key terms with a yellow highlighter works well to create the Skills section of the resume, as well as to construct the body of the e-mail cover letter.

Education and Certifications Educational accomplishments should be included on the resume. The emphasis that you choose to give to the resume determines where you will place the Education Section. Some feel that it should appear immediately after the Summary Statement. However, if presenting a functional resume or skills-based resume, where the skill set does not depend on the degree, or where the degree is quite unrelated, you may wish to place education after skills.

Certifications are equally important, especially in technical trades. Often many college degrees, even graduate degrees, are accompanied by certifications. Because of the technical nature of the job market, even with a general undergraduate degree technical certifications complement the degree and are a necessary entry into industry. For example, a four-year accounting degree is greatly enhanced by having certifications and experience with accounting software packages such as QuickBooks or Intuit industry certifications. Industry certifications are important because they are standardized by industry, whereas educational degrees have some degree of variance depending on the institution. Industry certifications are also very current. Finally, they are recognized by industry. The more industry certifications you possess the more competitive you will be in the job market.

Many are confused by the format that the educational section should take. The rule of thumb is that you should list the most recent and/or the highest degree received first, which typically is the most recent degree. However, if you have returned to school to pursue a particular set of industry-based skills, or other related certifications, those should be listed first. Always list the degree first, then the major, then the college or institution conferring the degree or certification, and finally the date. Include the Grade Point Average (GPA) if it is high (above a 3.75). Pertinent additional information may be included as well, as in the example below. A practice in previous years for older workers was not to include the date of their college degree in order to conceal their age and avoid age discrimination. This practice is not common or recommended, as an employer wants to see actual dates that you held jobs, as well as dates that you attended college. Job placement specialists are adamant about seeing the chronology of the dates and they do not want to see any dates missing.

The Education section for a business professional may look like this:

Education
M.A., Business Administration, XYZ College, New York, NY. 1993. GPA: 4.0/4.0.
B.A., Business, XYZ College, Minneapolis, MN, 1991. GPA: 3.89/4.0.

■ Professional Experience

Key Accomplishments

The employer is engaged and interested in the clean format of your resume, the well-written and succinct Summary of Qualifications, and the Skills section that shows you possess many of the sought after talents; and now it's time to show more depth in terms of work history. Current job placement specialists want to see a contextual and quantified presentation of your work history. As fashioned below, you will open with the position title, the name of the company, the city, and years. Then follow that opening with several sentences or phrases that clearly describe in industry terms what you did on a daily or weekly basis in that position. This requires thinking and rethinking—writing and rewriting—to synthesize the many job duties that you performed into organized categorical segments of that job. You will use these job duty "segments" to quantify your "key accomplishments." Remember, we mentioned earlier in the text that in industry, education, and other nonprofit organizations, proving or quantifying what you have done or accomplished is paramount to showing success. Start with the most recent job first. Even if the jobs are not entirely related, find a way to extract skills from that job that relate to the current position. An accurate and complete chronology of dates is very important for employers to follow. If the date is not included, potential employers may think you are trying to hide something. However, if there are jobs that are unrelated that you have held for a short time, you do not need to include them. There are many opinions on the issue of the format of resumes and whether to make a functional resume or a chronological resume. The opinions and standards change frequently, especially given rapidly changing technology, which directly impacts the form and delivery methods of the resume. This author, given her research and expert opinion from years of experience writing resumes, prefers a functional-based resume, with the skills summary presented first, followed by the job history section with positions presented in chronological order, most recent first. The Education section should be placed to reflect the emphasis you want to give it in relation to job skills, so decide if it is more or less important than skills and list if before or after the Skills section accordingly.

For a Sole Proprietor/Chiropractor, the Professional Experience section would look like the following example.

However, be careful. This is a template from Microsoft Office, found when you type "functional resume." Use this as a template, but craft it to reflect your very own experience. Something an employer does not want to find is this exact resume listed for many applicants, found simply by Googling a portion of the job history section.

■ Sample Functional Resume Template before Personalizing

Professional Experience

Communication: Reports/Presentations/Technology

- Prepare complex reports for managed care organizations and insurance companies, ensuring full compliance with agency requirements and tight deadlines

▨ Author professional correspondence to customers and vendors

▨ Design and deliver series of classes for local businesses and associations, providing ergonomic counseling and educating employees on proper lifting techniques to avoid injury

▨ Conduct small-group sessions on meditation/relaxation techniques

▨ Communicate medical concepts to patients using layman's terms to facilitate understanding

▨ Rapidly learn and master varied computer programs; recently completed Microsoft Office Suite certificate course

Customer Service/Marketing/Problem Solving

▨ Oversee front-office operations and provide impeccable customer service:

   ■ Built a clientele supported by 60% referral business

▨ Develop and implement strategic marketing plan for business:

   ■ Launched a thriving private practice, building revenue from $0 to over $72K in first three years with minimal overhead

   ■ Create special promotions, write/design print and outdoor advertising, and coordinate all media buying

▨ Won over a highly skeptical medical community as the first chiropractor to target MDs for informative in-service demonstrations, classes, and booths:

   ■ Presentations resulted in standing-room-only crowds of 50+

   ■ Increased client base by one-third resulting from MD referrals

   ■ ABC MASTERY & Organization

▨ Manage all aspects of day-to-day operations as multi-site owner and practitioner of Reynolds' Chiropractic:

   ■ Facility rental/maintenance

   ■ Patient scheduling for busy office averaging 52 appointments weekly

   ■ Finances: accounts payable/receivable, invoicing, insurance billing, budgeting

- Supervision of a total of eight medical receptionist interns

- Compliance with all healthcare facility, HMO, and insurance requirements

■ Sample Functional Resume Template after Personalizing and Embedding Key Accomplishments

Changes:

- Added job title, company name and address, and years of employment

- Reordered or prioritized job duties to focus on company ownership duties

- Used stronger descriptors

- Changed verbs to job phrases, to avoid having to use past and present tense verbs in the same sentence or paragraph

- Converted all retained verbs to present tense

- Deleted all periods where bullets are used

Professional Experience
Doctor of Chiropractor/Owner. ABC Company. San Diego, CA. 2000-2012.

Creative Marketing/Client Retention/Customer Service
Won over a highly skeptical medical community as the first chiropractor to target MDs for informative in-service demonstrations, classes, and booths:
  - Key Accomplishments:
    - Presentations resulted in standing-room-only crowds of 50+
    - Four MDs subsequently became patients
    - Increased client base by one-third resulting from MD referrals
Strategic marketing:
  - Key Accomplishment:
    - Launched a thriving private practice, building revenue from $0 to over $72K in first three years with minimal overhead
Special promotions
  - Key Accomplishments:
    - Wrote, designed and printed outdoor advertising
    - Coordinated all media buying to reduce costs by 40%
Front-office operations; impeccable customer service:
  - Key Accomplishments:
    - Built a clientele supported by 60% referral business
    - Accurately managed all aspects of accounting/bookkeeping and streamlined office operations

FIGURE 3 *Professional Experience section in Word format.*

▨ Increased white space for readability

▨ Focused on Key Accomplishments

▨ Deleted last two sections, which seemed to reiterate many of the accomplishments and duties listed in the first section—all related to the same job

In summary, what we see in this section is a blending of chronological Professional Experience with a Key Accomplishments section embedded contextually within the related job description, in line with the current paradigm of quantifying accomplishments.

References The reference section of the resume has been moved off of the resume as it really did not provide any real data, but rather read "Provided Upon Request." If the position asks that you provide references, then you should. But include them on a separate page. The full name, title, address, phone, and e-mail addresses should be included. Three references is usually sufficient. This page should be formatted in the same font and style as the resume.

Professional Experience

Doctor of Chiropractor/Owner. ABC Company. San Diego, CA. 2000-2012.

CREATIVE MARKETING/CLIENT RETENTION/CUSTOMER SERVICE
  Won over a highly skeptical medical community as the first chiropractor to target MDs for informative in-service demonstrations, classes, and booths:
      ○ Key Accomplishments:
          ▫ Presentations resulted in standing-room-only crowds of 50+
          ▫ Four MDs subsequently became patients
          ▫ Increased client base by one-third resulting from MD referrals
  Strategic marketing:
      ○ Key Accomplishment:
          ▫ Launched a thriving private practice, building revenue from $0 to over $72K in first three years with minimal overhead
  Special promotions
      ○ Key Accomplishments:
          ▫ Wrote, designed and printed outdoor advertising
          ▫ Coordinated all media buying to reduce costs by 40%
  Front-office operations; impeccable customer service:
      ○ Key Accomplishments:
          ▫ Built a clientele supported by 60% referral business
          ▫ Accurately managed all aspects of accounting/bookkeeping and streamlined office operations

FIGURE 4 *Professional Experience section in PDF format.*

REFERENCES

Mr. Joe Smith

Owner, Smith Chiropractic
1234 Meditation Lane
Pleasantville, IN 09878
Phone: 555-555-1212
E-mail: <u>jsm@yahoo.com</u>

■ **Mid-chapter Student Activity 8.3**
Based on the ideal job that you chose to seek in student Activities 8.1 & 8.2, create your: 1) Personal Information and 2) Professional Experience sections, including Key Accomplishments.

Formatting the Resume

Ah, the format of the resume. One page, two pages? What font? Spacing? Punctuation? Is it really that important? The answer to all these questions is "Yes." All of these factors are extremely important. So let's talk about what the employer wants to see on the resume. Then we will address what the employer does not want to see on the resume.

Again, remember that resumes are electronic. Therefore, the first thing that the employer is going to see is not you, but your resume. In fact, before seeing the resume the employer will see the title of the resume in the subject line of the e-mail, so even the convention for naming the resume is extremely important.

Again, remember that employers spend as little as ten seconds on their first scan of your resume. And it is truly just that—a scan. Some current Internet studies suggest that recruiters spend as little as six seconds on your resume (Giang, www.linkedin.com). This site discusses a study that used scientific eye tracking to show a heat map of where the recruiters' eyes moved during their brief resume scans. The resume that was formatted according to the practices that we are discussing in this chapter captured more of the attention of the eye. The cleaner the format, the more in line with what employers are expecting to see, the more in depth the eye movement will be, as the pertinent information will be easier to find.

What the Employer Wants to See on the Resume:

- A One-Page Resume

- Bulleted Items, not lenghty narrative paragraphs

- Key Accomplsihments embedded contextually in Professional Experience

- Quantified Skills and Accomplishments

- A readable font such as Arial, Cambria, or Times New Roman in 10 or 12 point font

- Single or 1.15 spacing for paragraphs, double spacing between paragraphs or something comparable

- Typographically and grammatically error free copy

- Inclusion of dates for job experience, certifications, and degrees

- Computer and technolgy skills, specified

- References on a Separate Page

What the Employer Does Not Want to See on the Resume:

- "Job Objective"—Use a "Professional Summary Statement" instead

- Irrelevant Jobs—short, and irrelevant jobs should be omitted

- Lengthy Narrative Paragraphs

- Typographical or Grammatical Errors. Turn on Spellchecker, Grammar, and Style Checker. Put the resume down, read it the next day. Have a friend read it. You will find the errors this way. It is difficult for each of us to see our own errors, as our mind's ideas do not us allow to see what is on the page.

- Personal Information and Hobbies—just do not include them.

- References—only provide them if asked, and on a separate page.

- An unprofessional e-mail account—create a new professional one—it's free. Use your name and a few numbers to differentiate it.

- Be consistent and professional with the name that you use for your e-mail account, the resume, the portfolio, and the subject line. These are the first things the employer sees in the e-mail that she/he is opening.

- No need to include "Phone" or "E-mail" in front of them—it's obvious

- Your current employer's information

- No pictures or graphics, they will not scan well

What the Employer May Want to See An employer may want to see a photo or even a video portfolio of you in certain occupations, such as radio, TV, film, modeling, acting, or graphic design. You should know your particular industry and look for sample resumes and portfolios if this is the case. If so, there are sites that support this type of portfolio. Even LinkedIn includes a section where you can upload a PowerPoint portfolio that employers can view on your LinkedIn site. Alert your potential employer to this information when you are contacting them in response to a job ad. Sites such as www.LinkedIn.com, www.pinterest.com and others not only give access to upload resumes, but also to upload portfolios and videos. Use them judiciously.

The Electronic Career Portfolio (EPortfolio)

It is important to know that the first place an employer will go to check your online presence is Google; the second place they will go to check your online portfolio is LinkedIn. Many employers will also check your Facebook account. Though not entirely embraced, this practice is legal and common. LinkedIn IS your electronic portfolio. Make sure that the resume that you would submit via e-mail matches the profile that you create on LinkedIn and other social networking sites.

The electronic portfolio is becoming a more accepted and expected way to show an employer your skills in some arenas. In fields where creativity is valued, these can work well for the candidate.

A conservative approach to a PowerPoint portfolio might include the following:

- Your Personal Information on Slide One

- The Professional Summary Statement on Slide Two

- Your Job Skills on Slide Three

- Professional Summary on Slides Four, Five, and Six, depending on length

- Scanned copies of Industry Certifications and Awards on subsequent slides

- Scanned Letters of Reference on the next few slides—limit them to three

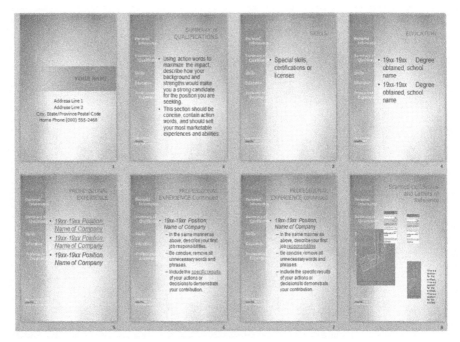

FIGURE 5 *The electronic PowerPoint portfolio.*

If you are proficient with editing software, you could even turn the Power-Point slideshow into a video to show an employer spontaneously at a job fair and upload it to your Pinterest.com pin board site.

A field that demands more creativity may accept resumes that are very different, and that use graphic design to create a portfolio that is more infused with text boxes and graphics. These are becoming increasingly popular. You should keep it honest and interesting and brand yourself. Use the same or a similar graphic and color design and scheme on all pieces that you present to the employer: business card, the resume, a PowerPoint show, an online Personal Portfolio, and even the e-mail that you send. The background of that e-mail, the name that you use for the Website address and e-mail address, should all match, as the more common threads the employer sees, the more easily the employer can create a visual image or "brand" of you.

Building an online portfolio is essential for designers, artists, photographers, and developers. Fortunately, there are numerous sites on the Internet that will help you do just that. WordPress is an excellent choice, incorporating blogging capabilities, social networking, and contact information with professional portfolio designs and templates to showcase your work. Simply searching for online or electronic portfolios will net countless results and much expert advice.

The Old-School Portfolio

The New Online Electronic Personal Portfolio

Removing the First Potential Roadblock: Writing a Winning Cover Letter

The format and content of the "cover letter"—in a traditional or "e-mail cover letter" format, cannot be overemphasized. It is a critical component in the job application package. What many applicants fail to realize is that the cover letter is the first piece of writing that the employer reads. It is the employer's first introduction to you. Often a job seeker spends so much time on the resume, that when she discovers she will need to personalize each cover letter for every job she applies for, it feels overwhelming. But to be successful in the job search process, the applicant must capture the attention of the employer in the cover letter. It is important that the person placing the ad feels that the applicant has not only read the qualifications carefully but that the person is able to demonstrate, job skill by job skill, the qualifications that match that skill.

The cover letter is THE "First Impression."

Moreover, the employer is looking very carefully to see that you are responding specifically to the requirements of their job ad.

A resume is a summary of your skills and experience.

A cover letter shows the employer that you can match the skills they are seeking to your qualifications, point by point.

If you can match your skills, extracting them from the resume in a narrative format, to the skills listed in the ad, and if you can do this in an organized, cohesive, and compelling fashion, you are removing one of the roadblocks to receiving serious consideration from your potential employer in the form of an interview.

A cover letter introduces you to the potential employer and should offer information specific to the job ad. Traditionally, a cover letter would be sent with the resume in hard copy format. This practice still exists in some larger organizations, and educational or government settings. However, the practice is changing fast as most applications are filled out online and the entire "job application package" is delivered via e-mail. Still, in these more traditional settings, the cover letter, though written and delivered electronically, should be written in a traditional business letter format.

A skill that is not often emphasized in high school or college settings is writing a formal business letter. However, you will find excellent examples online and in business writing and communication textbooks.

Traditional Cover Letter

Current Date

Title, First Name, Last Name
Company Name
City, State Zip Code

Recipient Title, First Name, Last Name
Company Name
City, State Zip Code

Dear Title, Last Name:

Capture the attention of the reader in this opening paragraph! Start with a strong opening sentence. Paragraph one is the introductory paragraph and it is the first paragraph the recipient will read, so it is very important, just like first impressions. Here you introduce the recipient to your reason for sending the correspondence and summarize what you are going to address.

Paragraph two should be the longest paragraph, because it should contain the ideas that you introduced in paragraph one, but with supporting examples and with detail. Pay attention to the order of informational items. Bring the topics up in paragraph two in the order that you introduced them in paragraph one. State the topic or assertion, and then follow with a supporting example. Conclude paragraph two with a nice transitional line that flows into paragraph three.

This concluding paragraph typically thanks the recipient for taking the time to review the information carefully, and then asks for action by stating that you are looking forward to meeting them or hearing from them soon.

Closing,

Title, First Name, Last Name
Typist's initials, lower case

FIGURE 6 *Block style business letter template.*

In the example above, we can see suggestions for writing any effective business letter. These same formatting and content rules apply when creating a cover letter to specifically address a job ad.

Start with an introductory paragraph, introduce yourself as a qualified candidate, then develop paragraph two with specific examples of how your skills and experience meet the qualifications of the job.

Finally, thank the employer for reviewing your materials and state that you are looking forward to joining the team. It sounds standard and simple, right? But many struggle with this very important job application piece of writing.

Use the techniques described below to write a winning cover letter!

E-mail Cover Letter The e-mail cover letter is the most common way to respond to a job ad. You will be creating the e-mail to introduce yourself, attaching your resume in a Word or PDF format, and you may direct the employer to LinkedIn, WordPress, or other online portfolios that you may have.

Before writing the cover letter and resume, you must educate yourself regarding job skills required by employers. In this way, you can tailor your skills and experience on your resume to meet those skills listed in the job ads. "Craigslist.org" has become the dynamic and "advertising free" conduit between employee and employer. Also, using Craigslist, you can specify which local town or city area of a larger metropolis you are interested in. The layout is simple, "grass roots," and very reflective of real jobs that employers need to have filled immediately.

A myriad of job posting sites can be found by simply Googling "Job Search and Interviewing Skills" to locate current sources. Ladders.com, Monster.com, Craigslist.org, and many other sites on the Internet are excellent resources for all aspects of the job search process.

Once you have found your ads, underline the key skills the employer is seeking. You will respond to them in order in your cover letter.

A three-paragraph cover letter will work well. Work offline first, then copy and paste your finished Word file into the body of the e-mail. Save the cover letter for use with future jobs. You can then just tailor it to fit each different position.

A few specific considerations with an e-mail cover letter involve the Date and Subject Line. The date does not need to be typed in an e-mail cover letter, as it is already included in the e-mail header. Also, the Subject Line should contain your name and the job number, ID, or title. The company address does not need to be included either, as you are directing this to an e-mail address.

Open with Dear Sir or Madam, or Dear Hiring Manager, unless a specific name is provided. Often in our modern workplace, it is not.

E-mail Memorandum Style Job Search Cover Letter

TO: JaneDoe@abc.net

FROM: jmartin@123.net

Cc: pertinentparty@456.net, 2ndpertinentparty@456.net

Bcc: hrmanager@123.net

SUBJECT: Job Title, or Job Posting ID Number

Dear Title Last Name:

Capture the attention of the reader in this opening paragraph! Use language from the Summary Statement on the Resume. Start with a strong opening sentence. Paragraph one is the introductory paragraph and it is the first paragraph the recipient will read, so it is very important, just like first impressions. Here you introduce the recipient to your reason for sending the correspondence and summarize what you are going to address.

Paragraph two should be the longest paragraph, because it should contain the ideas that you introduced in paragraph one, but with supporting examples and with detail. Pay attention to the order of informational items. Bring the job skills topics up in paragraph two in the order that you introduced them in paragraph one. State the topic or assertion, and then follow with a supporting example of the skills and qualifications that you possess. Conclude paragraph two with a nice transitional line that flows into paragraph three.

This concluding paragraph typically thanks the recipient for taking the time to review the information carefully, and then asks for action by stating that you are looking forward to meeting them or hearing from them soon. Provide the best contact phone number.

Closing,

Title, First Name, Last Name
Phone, extension

FIGURE 7 *E-mail Memorandum template for job search cover letter. Single or double space paragraphs, include Greeting and Closing Lines*

Write a very compelling, engaging, interesting opening paragraph, styled after your Summary Statement. Using language from the Summary of Qualifications Statement from the resume creates consistency for the employer while reading your materials.

Move into paragraph two, citing examples from the job ads and matching them with your specific job skills, work history, and education. Stating the job skill, then providing supporting examples from your resume, will show the employer you have carefully worked through the position requirements and thoughtfully pinpointed how you meet those qualifications.

Close with a complimentary thank you for reviewing your qualifications and provide the best phone number or e-mail address to contact you. If you have taken your time with this part of the application process, it will greatly enhance your chances of being called for an interview!

■ Student Activity 8.4

Directions:

1. The Cover Letter

   Log on to Craigslist.org and search job ads based on a job title or area that you are interested in or for which you feel qualified.

   Print three or four ads, highlight the skills listed, and keep these. You will need to refer to them when completing the body of the e-mail message, which has your resume attached.

   Study the ads, many of them, in depth. Compare the qualifications employers are seeking, the pay, duties, and any other special qualifications.

   Then use one of the ads to create an e-mail cover letter similar to the example in this chapter above.

2. The Resume

   Using the ad and cover letter above, craft your resume to apply for this particular job. You may use the pieces created from the mid-chapter activities to construct your resume, adding any missing pieces, and tailoring it to fit this position.

Chapter Eight

Are You Prepared for Today's Job Search?

Job Search Strategies and the Interview Process

© Stephen Coburn, 2012. Used under license from Shutterstock, Inc.

Chapter Eight

Learning Objectives

LO1 Describe the importance of Digital Information Literacy for Job Readiness.

LO2 Describe the importance of Assessments and Certifications to prepare for the job.

LO3 Identify Job Search strategies.

LO4 Explain the importance of Informal Networks.

LO5 Respond appropriately to the Most Frequently Asked Interview Questions.

LO6 Describe Interview Formats.

LO7 Describe the importance of Job Interview Follow-Up.

ow that you have a winning resume, e-portfolio, and effective cover letter, you need to consider how to navigate the interview process. As with any major pursuit in life, this requires research to know expectations, some strategic planning, and preparation. In addition, as with deciding on a format for a resume, cover letter, and portfolio, there are copious examples online and in business communication and related textbooks that will discuss in depth how to prepare before and for the interview, as well as how to follow-up after the interview. Also, when searching for information online, make sure the information is current, so include a date. An effective strong search would be "job search strategies 2012."

Digital Information Literacy

Digital information literacy refers to the ability of a person to locate, evaluate, assess, and integrate information into meaningful content. If a job seeker does not already possess these skills, it makes the job search process much more difficult. In many applications used in today's business arena, it is imperative and expected that workers are computer and information literate. The standards are high. Employees are expected to know the Office Suite: Word, Excel, Access, PowerPoint, and Outlook, to a high level of proficiency. Further, workers need to know how to search the Internet for meaningful data and then interpret data in a form that may be sent as a message or posted to the Internet as a form, database, or Website. As well, they are asked to download that information locally so that it can be used in Word to prepare a report; in PowerPoint to give an oral presentation or for e-mail or an online viewing; in Access to manage records; or Excel to show significant company data in a quantitative fashion, or to show trends and processes. These skills are highly under-recognized by job seekers and even by academic institutions, and there are no real formal assessments conducted on a large and consistent scale that test for individuals' digital literacy skills.

However, the important point to remember is that employers expect you to have these skills. Therefore, before moving into the interview process, it is paramount to assess your current digital information literacy skills. Fortunately, there are agencies and educational institutions that provide excellent services to help in this assessment and training, if you wish to upgrade your skills.

Assessments and Certifications as an Integral Part of the Interview Process

Assessments

Assessing your skills in a quantifiable manner is an important part of the interview preparation process. Employers will often test you on a particular software package as part of the interview process. In certain organizations, a typing test from a recognized institution is required. Additionally, software skills, basic writing and math skills, and business letter composition skills are also tested before the actual interview. If you have listed on your resume that you are an expert QuickBooks or Excel user, you may be tested on those particular software packages. Therefore, it is best to assess yourself, *before* trying to sell yourself to an employer. If you are deficient in any of these very important digital information literacy skills, then you can address it before the interview process begins.

Staffing agencies are particularly helpful in assessing your software skills. By setting up an appointment or an interview with an agency, you are able to take its software exams. Many agencies, such as Accountemps and Manpower, offer hundreds of software tests, and the opportunity to retest if the initial score was not high enough. Community colleges and career centers are also low cost avenues to acquire job skills. These are also excellent sources to review your resume, to make suggestions, and to engage you in the interview process.

Social networking skills cannot be overlooked as an emerging and critical skill set. The ability to use Facebook, Twitter, LinkedIn, Pinterest, and other popular social networking sites are skill sets that are becoming increasingly expected in many occupations as well. To become more adept at these skills, you can simply set up a free Website or blog on one of thousands of sites, and add these tools to your site. Then start posting!

In fact, a new study is even citing Facebook as a better predictor of college and career success than standardized tests used by human resources departments worldwide (Huppke, 2012). The results are to be published soon in the *Journal of Applied Social Psychology.* Employers have long been known to use Facebook as a way to scan to eliminate someone who was doing something inappropriate. Now they may be able to use it to predict the success of a potential candidate.

Certifications

Certifications strengthen the job search package. If you have a Bachelor's Degree or even a Master's Degree, but return to college to take additional online or evening classes in an area that will strengthen your degree or add recency to that degree or job skill set, you will strengthen your chances of getting hired.

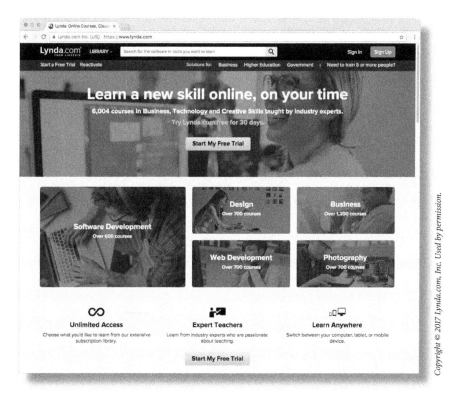

FIGURE 1 *Online Software Training*

Employers value digital literacy and job readiness certificates. Certiport is one such global certification program that offers testing in an IC3 credential. Certiport also provides the "official Microsoft Office certification programs, the Microsoft Technology Associate certification program, the Adobe® Certified Associate certification program, the Autodesk Certified User program, the CompTIA Strata™ IT Fundamentals, and the Intuit QuickBooks Certified User certification program" (Certiport, 2009).

Lynda.com is an online training site that offers training in hundreds of business and computer skills such as: 3D Animation, Audio, Design, Developer Skills, Business Creating Documentaries, Home Computing, Photography, and Video and Web technologies. Once you have completed the training, you receive a Certificate of Completion that can be delivered a number of different ways. You can choose to save it as a PDF and print it, you can e-mail the Certificate of Completion to one or more individuals, or you can even embed it into a Web page, to show your friends and current or potential employer the value of your newly acquired skills.

Pursuing current certifications clearly makes a difference in today's fast changing technological job market. Employers will value your skill set with these competitive cutting edge digital information literacy abilities and certifications.

Job Search Strategies

Active and Passive Job Search   A rather recent development in the job search process is the ability to post your resume online. This "passive" technique allows the database to "match" your job skills with the job skills that the employer has specified in the job ad and has also uploaded to the job site. This is one more reason why it is important to use standard industry jargon to describe your skill set. If your skill set language is not the same as that posted by the employer, no match will be found. However, if your skills match, an auto-generated or employer-generated e-mail will be sent to you. At this point, you are now in contact with the employer directly and you may send your resume, cover letter, and e-portfolio.

Active job search also involves a job database, but the resume is not uploaded to the site. Instead, the job seeker searches the job database site using keywords such as job title or job skills. The job applicant goes through a series of steps to sign up for the particular service, such as at Monster.com. A user profile is created with a username and password. You are then able to search for jobs, find a job ad that interests you, and send your resume as an attachment directly to the employer, via e-mail.

Your chances of being asked for an interview will continue to increase if you engage in both practices—both posting your resume to the job database site so that the database is making the match and looking actively by using keyword search terms.

Monster.com was one of the first sites to allow users to upload their resumes for employers to view. Monster has one of the best "resume builders" available online. For those not accustomed to resume creation, it will walk you through each section of the process. It is tedious and time consuming to fill in all of the sections, but it is an excellent tool. You can also cut and paste from an already created resume, or upload a Word file. If you build your resume online, it is important to complete each section thoroughly and to be accurate with spelling and grammar. The .org site Craigslist.org has become very popular worldwide as a site that represents both local and global employers. It has a grassroots look and feel, rather than a corporate presence with ads like many other sites.

The use of a job database and the need to "upload" your electronic resume file are primary reasons that resumes should be kept simple. A screen friendly font such as Arial or Cambria is preferred, and there should be no lines or graphic symbols on the resume, because this will prevent it from being uploaded properly to the job search database.

Networking   *Informal Networks*

In spite of the tremendous amount of virtual communication that takes place on the Web today, including social networking, and the use of electronic resumes and portfolios, the most effective way to land the job interview is still networking through friends, colleagues, and acquaintances, essentially by word of mouth or e-mail. These contacts must be developed. It is surprising how large the network can become when you start to let everyone know that you are looking for a job.

Also, you can search using more formal networks. These include joining professional organizations, and going to business meetings and social events. Post your resume to job forums and message boards online. Before you do this though, make sure that your job search package is complete, that your letters of reference are current, and that you are ready for the inquiries that are sure to come your way.

The Interview

After assessing your skills, you now have a realistic picture of what you can sell to an employer. By engaging in the assessment process, it is highly likely that you have also gathered skills regarding how to speak about your certifications and training. This will assist you in the interview process. Now you have to put these skills and the attractive resume and portfolio package to effective use. This can be one of the most anxiety-ridden parts of the job search. As we mentioned before, fear of public speaking is the number one fear in America. Fear of speaking in front of a panel of interviewers, or even one interviewer, can be frightening as well.

Fortunately, there are many sources of information that you can turn to that will help alleviate those fears and prepare you to speak confidently with your potential employer. One of the most important aspects to this stage of the job search process is to practice answering the questions that you will likely encounter. Job search seminars and workshops are found in every city. Also, have friends and family ask you the questions from a script. It is essential that you hear yourself speak the answers to these questions a few times before the actual interview. If you have practiced within a day or so before the interview, this script will be fresh in your mind, so that in spite of your nervous feelings, the answers will come readily to the forefront of your memory.

What are the most common questions that an interviewer will ask you?

1. So tell me about yourself.

2. Why did you leave your last job?

3. What did you not like about your previous employer?

4. What are your greatest strengths?

5. What are your weaknesses?

6. If your previous coworkers were here, what would they say about you?

7. A customer calls to complain and asks for your supervisor. What do you do?

8. A customer is irate on the phone or in the office. How would you handle this?

9. Where else are you applying?

10. Do you prefer to work alone?

11. Are you willing to put the needs of XYZ Company ahead of your own?

12. What do you know about our company?

13. Let's talk about salary.

14. Are you willing to work overtime?

15. Why should I hire you?

16. Do you have any questions to ask me?

■ **Mid-chapter Student Activity 1**

For this activity, all students should have their resumes and portfolios from Chapter Eight in hand.

Your partner is your neighbor to your right. Using this tear out page, have one person be the interviewee and the other the interviewer. Take turns asking half of the questions to one another. Answer the questions to the best of your ability given your current knowledge of the interviewing process. Write the responses down carefully, exchanging the tear out sheet when the roles change halfway through the questions.

Answers to the most common questions that an interviewer will ask you.

Now it is time to consider the most appropriate answers to these questions.

1. **So tell me about yourself.**

   This is a question that most employers ask to initiate the conversation. But it is very open ended so be careful. Respond to this question with an answer that talks about your *professional* self, not your personal self.

2. **Why did you leave your last job?**

   Remain positive with this question. Do not state that it is for more money, even though it may be. This question is best answered by stating that you wish to advance your career.

3. **What did you not like about your previous employer?**

   Again, keep it positive. State that it was not because you did not like your last employer. You are looking for career advancement and increasing opportunity.

4. **What are your greatest strengths?**

   Now this is the question that you should have well rehearsed in your mind. This is your chance to shine. Talk about why you are a great employee. Do not use standard, cliché answers though such as "I'm a great team player." Have this answer well formulated and talk about your unique skills and abilities.

5. **What are your weaknesses?**

   This is a very difficult question, but you cannot say that you do not have any weaknesses. You will need to choose a small example of a weakness, such as being so open to new design ideas that you may sometimes be entertaining too many choices and need to focus on fewer choices before making a final decision.

6. **If your previous coworkers were here, what would they say about you?**

   Again, this could be a question that elicits an honest response, and that response might include a co-worker who perhaps you had conflict with. But, keep it positive and think about what the coworkers that you had synergy with would say.

7. **A customer calls to complain, and asks for your supervisor. What do you do?**

   The interviewer is most likely trying to see if you are self-reliant enough to try to resolve the complaint on your own, and keep the supervisor from having to manage it for you. You want to assure the interviewer that you will do everything possible at your line of delegated duty to please the customer.

8. **A customer is irate on the phone or in the office. How would you handle this?**

   You do not want to answer that you hung up on them! Again, the interviewer is trying to see if you know how to calm the customer and continue to maintain your professionalism.

9. **Where else are you applying?**

   "I have just started the process . . ." would be a safe answer to this question. You do not want potential employers who know one another in a specific industry to be comparing notes.

10. **Do you prefer to work alone?**

    Make sure you let the employer know that you are comfortable both working in teams and alone.

11. **Are you willing to put the needs of XYZ Company ahead of your own?**

    This is really an unfair question, but an employer may ask it anyhow. If you answer "Yes" then you may seem to not care about family. If you answer "No" then you do not care about the company. Use an answer that lets the interviewer know that you are confident that you can create balance in your life between company and family life and that you work very hard in both arenas.

12. **What do you know about our company?**

    This is not a trick question. It is a fair one. Before coming to the interview, make sure you have researched the company and can speak intelligently about it.

13. **Let us talk about salary.**

It is too early in the first interview for either the interviewer or interviewee to be speaking about salary. But if the question comes your way, be prepared. Go to www.salary.com before the interview, know the market and what you should be asking for in this position. Hopefully, you will come close to getting what comparable jobs in the area pay.

14. **Are you willing to work overtime?**

This can be a working condition, so this is may be a tricky question as well. State that you are willing to do what it takes to get the job done and if overtime is required at times, you again are willing to do what it takes to get the job done.

15. **Why should I hire you?**

Again, this is another question where you can shine! Let the employer see that you truly believe that you are the best candidate for this job, that you are enthusiastic about joining the team, that your talents will fit this position perfectly, and that you are looking forward to beginning.

16. **Do you have any questions to ask me?**

A question that I love in response to the interviewer's question is "What would a typical day be like on this job?" Also, you could ask: "Is there any question that you would like to clarify further?" or "What is the team that I would be assigned to working on presently?" This is your chance to end the interview on a level that shows that you are curious, still engaged in the interview, and eager to start.

Interview Formats They are several different types of interviews that you may encounter. They range from formal to informal and from one-on-one to group interviews. Competition is toughest when there are many qualified candidates competing for the same job. During these times, employers can get quite creative in their interview formats.

The one-on-one interview is the most traditional format. In a one-on-one interview, you and your potential employer are getting to know one another directly. The format of the questions may vary in this type of interview. Some companies will design the interview questions to see how you react under stress. This type of interview does not occur much anymore. Instead, situational or behavioral interviews are used. In situational interviews, you are asked hypothetical questions, and asked how you would react to a situation. In contrast, a behavioral interview relies on questions that are specifically based on your past performance. In this case, the interviewer has become familiar with your resume and portfolio before you enter the room. This is a very effective type of interview format for the employer and is widely used.

A panel interview is common also, especially in a larger organization. Often there will be a common script that all participants have in front of them. The interviewers take turns asking questions from this script and do not deviate from it. This creates equity among candidates in the interview process. Make sure that when you are answering questions you establish direct eye contact with the person asking the question, then move to other interviewers with your eyes and responses so that everyone feels included.

An increasingly common interview is the phone interview. This saves both the interviewer and interviewee time. Phone presence, having a pleasant tone on the phone, answering professionally, and being prepared for the questions are equally important in the phone interview. Have your resume and cover letter in front of you before this interview as well.

Salary and Benefits Interviewing also involves discussing salary and benefits at some point in the process. However, it is best to wait until the second interview to discuss these issues, unless the interviewer asks you during the interview about your target salary range.

This is also an area that merits preparation. You should have knowledge of a salary range by having done some research in the area. Salaries can vary widely given differences in location, company size, and culture, so make sure that you have done your homework, and that you are placing yourself in a realistic salary bracket. There will be a chance to negotiate the salary during the interview.

Benefits are not offered as liberally in a difficult economy, so an employer may offer benefits only after a three- or six-month evaluation with positive results. It is appropriate however, to ask about benefits, once the job has been offered to you.

Follow-up It often makes a difference to follow-up on a job after the interview by sending a handwritten thank you note or an e-mail, and calling about a week or two after the interview to check on the status of the job. An employer that receives a thank you note will notice this, as it unusual for many interviewers to follow-up in this fashion. Especially if the candidates interviewed are comparable in their qualifications, following up, by trying to keep a relationship going with the company, the receptionist, and the people that you interviewed with, is critical. Do not let them forget you. Remember, employers in a tough economy are sometimes choosing from hundreds of qualified candidates so you have to engage in this type of follow-up to let them know you are still interested in the position.

Continued Career Development In a very changing information age, it is imperative that you continue to develop yourself professionally. Continue to take courses in areas related to your career to help you advance. Also, remain current with fast changing technologies. Finally, know your competition. Compare your skills, abilities, and accomplishments with what others in your area are doing, and, at the very least, compete at their level. To advance, consider how you can distinguish yourself from your competition. As you improve, update your resume and portfolio with the workshops, seminars, classes, certifications, and degrees that you pursue. Note any awards received as well.

As always, stay on the cutting edge!

For More Information on Job Preparedness, see this author's text "The Last Little Job Finding Manual You'll Ever Need" https://he.kendallhunt.com/product/last-little-job-finding-manual-youll-ever-need-removing-roadblocks-job-search-process

Works Cited

n.d. *Cambridge Dictionaries Online.* 2 February 2012 <http://dictionary.cambridge.org/dictionary/british/idiom>.

n.d. *dictionary.reference.com.* Ed. Collins English Dictionary—Complete & Unabridged 10th Edition. HarperCollins Publishers. 30 March 2012 <http://dictionary.reference.com/browse/insidious>.

Barnlund, D. C. *A Transactional Model of Communication.* New Brunswick: Transaction, 2008.

———. "A Transactional Model of Communication." 1970.

Bennett, Dashiell. *on . . . Hillary Clinton On Gay Rights Abroad: Secretary Of State Delivers Historic LGBT Speech In Geneva.* 7 December 2011.

Berkes, Howard. "Challenger: Reporting a Disaster's Cold, Hard Facts." 28 January 2006. *www.npr.org.* 24 March 2012 <http://www.npr.org/templates/story/story.php?storyId=5175151>.

Berlo, D. K. *The Process of Communication.* New York: Holt, Rinehart, & Winston. 1960.

Boswell, Wendy. "boolean.htm." 2012. *http://websearch.about.com.* 21 March 2012 <http://websearch.about.com/od/internetresearch/a/boolean.htm>.

Burnes, James MacGregor. *Leadership.* New York: Harper & Row Publishers, Inc., 1978.

Certiport. "Certiport Who We Are." 15 July 2009. *certiport.com.* 14 April 2012 <www.certiport.com>.

Covington, David, et al. "Communication in the Workplace." August 2007. *courses.ncsu.edu.* 5 April 2012 <http://courses.ncsu.edu/eng331/common/resources/ciw2007/appd.html>.

Cuyler, Greta, editor. "NJ Residents Urged to Monitor Hazardous Weather, Potential Flood Conditions." *PrincetonPatch.* 17 May 2011.

Denison, Daniel R. and Aneil K. Mishra. "Toward a Theory of Organizational Culture and Effectiveness." *Organization Science* March–April 1995: 206.

Droppers, Kristi. "Engage employees with effective communications." 1 March 2006. *www.highbeam.com.* 7 November 2011 <http://www.highbeam.com/doc/1G1-144567865.html>.

Dubay, William H. "Readability." 2004. *www.nald.ca*. 5 February 2012 <http://www.nald.ca/library/research/readab/readab.pdf>.

Economist, The. "Women in the Workforce." 30th December 2009. *www.economist.com*. 28 January 2012 <http://www.economist.com/node/15174418>.

"Essay: The Cognitive Style of PowerPoint: Pitching Out Corrupts Within." n.d. *http://www.edwardtufte.com*. 2012 8 June <http://www.edwardtufte.com/tufte/books_pp>.

Figliola, Patricia Moloney. "Text and Multimedia Messaging: Emerging Issues for Congress." CRS Report for Congress. 2008.

Fisher, Dalmar. *Communication in Organizations.* Jaico Publishing House. 2006.

Garret, R. K., & Danziger, J. N. (2007). "IM=Interruption Management? Instant Messaging and Disruption in the Workplace." *Journal of Computer-Mediated Communication* (2007): 13(1), article 2.

Giang, Vivian. "What Recruiters Look At During The 6 Seconds They Spend On Your Resume." 9 April 2012. *www.linkedin.com*. 12 April 2012 <http://www.linkedin.com/news?actionBar=&articleID=5595149483949174869&ids=0Se30TdzAQdP8RejoRdjgPejkRb3AQdPsMcPgMdPsUdj4Pe3gVdjkIczATdj4Vd3wMcj8Rdz4TcPARdiMTdP0OcPgRe3kQdPwNe3gPejkRb3wOd3sMczcQcPsRcP8NdjkVdjkIejoUd3sNejgVcPwQejgNdjARdiMVcjkTcjwTd3kQdzAUdPw>.

Groth, Aimee. "One Third Of Employers Say They Can't Fill Jobs Because There Aren't Enough Qualified Candidates." 24 October 2011. *articles.businessinsider.com*. 30 March 2012 <http://articles.businessinsider.com/2011-10-24/strategy/30315592_1_employers-machine-operators-manpowergroup>.

Hardin, Jewell. "The Importance of Good Will." *Article Alley.* 2 December 2009.

Hollis, Karyn, et. al. *http://grammar.ccc.commnet.edu/grammar.* n.d. 20 February 2012 <jmcnamara@ccc.commnet.edu.>.

Home, Business & Work. http://www.squidoo.com/thecommunicationcycle n.d. *squidoo.com*. 9 November 2011 <http://www.squidoo.com/thecommunicationcycle>.

http://en.wikipedia.org/wiki/SMS. n.d. *Wikipedia.com*. 2 January 2012 <http://en.wikipedia.org/wiki/SMS>.

Huppke, Rex. "Facebook and Job Performance." 19 February 2012. *articles.chicagotribune.com*. 14 April 2012 <http://articles.chicagotribune.com/2012-02-19/business/ct-biz-0220-work-advice-huppke-20120219_1_facebook-page-job-success-social-networking>.

Information Please Database. "A0921862.html." 22 July 2008. *www.infoplease.com*. Source: Pew Internet & American Life Project tracking surveys. 21 March 2012 <http://www.infoplease.com/ipa/A0921862.html>.

Jacobson, David. "Interpreting Instant Messaging: Context and Meaning in Computer-Mediated Communication." *Journal of Anthropological Research Vol. 63*, No. 3 Fall 2007: 359–381.

Kahane, C. (1986). *An Evaluation of Child Passenger Safety: The Effectiveness And Benefits of Safety Seats.* Washington, D.C.: NHTSA Report Number DOT HS 806 890.

Kantor, Jonathan. "White Papers and Social Media: A Symbiotic Relationship." 2010. *www.whitepapersource.com.* 2 March 2012 <http://www.whitepapersource.com/marketing/white-papers-and-social-media-a-symbiotic-relationship/>.

Kaslow, Amy, and Pam Tate. "US Economy's Hidden Asset: Older Workers." *The Christian Science Monitor.* 14 February 2011: 1.

Klare, George R. *The Measurement of Readability.* Ames: Iowa State University Press. 1963.

Lewis, E. St. Elmo. ""Catch-Line and Argument." *The Book-Keeper.* February 1903: 124.

Lin, Lihui. "Sender and the Receiver Form Expectations of the Value of Knowledge Based on Their Information." University of Washington Business School. 2005.

MACEPA Path, Fighting Malaria Together Newsletter. "Dec10news_sms." December 2010. *Learning Community MACEPA Path.* 12 December 2011 <http://www.macepalearningcommunity.org/dec10news_sms.htm>.

Micciche, Laura R. *Making a Case for Rhetorical Grammar.* Vol. 55, No. 4. National Council of Teachers of English, 2004.

Milian, Mark. "invented-text-messaging.html." 3 May 2009. *latimesblog.latimes.com.* 21 2012 January <http://latimesblogs.latimes.com/technology/2009/05/invented-text-messaging.html>.

Milliken, Frances. "Milliken.Frances.pdf." 4 November 2003. *w4.stern.nyu.edu.* 30 March 2012 <http://w4.stern.nyu.edu/emplibrary/Milliken.Frances.pdf>.

n.p. "17% of Americans believe that using email increased their workload." 17 October 2008. *www.itfacts.biz.* 22 January 2012 <http://www.itfacts.biz/17-of-americans-believe-that-using-email-increased-their-workload/11708>.

———. *ClicheSite, Cliches, Euphemisms & Figures or Speech.* 27 January 2012.

———. "Online Advertising to Reach Nine Percent of Total Ad Spend by 2011." 24 July 2006. *www.marketingvox.com.* 2012 2 March <http://www.marketingvox.com/online_advertising_to_reach_nine_percent_of_total_ad_spend_by_2011-022249/>.

———. *Participles & Misplaced Modifiers atpppst.com.* 23 August 2011. 20 February 2012 <http://languagearts.pppst.com/dangling-participles.html>.

———. *Portable Document Format.* 15 March 2012. 16 May 2012 <http://en.wikipedia.org/wiki/Portable_Document_Format>.

Nichol, Mark. *7 Examples of Passive Voice (And How To Fix Them).* February 2011.

Ogaswara, Todd. "the-reason-for-the-160-character-text-message-and-140-character-twitter-length-limits_b3909." 4 May 2009. *socialtimes.com.* 21 January 2012 <http://socialtimes.com/the-reason-for-the-160-character-text-message-and-140-character-twitter-length-limits_b3909>.

p., n. "Best Fonts For On=Screen Use." Copyright © A3webtech 2002–2011. *www. a3webtech.com.* 14 January 2012 <http://www.a3webtech.com/index.php/best-fonts-onscreen.html>.

Patterson, Kerry, and Joseph Grenny, Ron McMillan, Al Switzler *Crucial Confrontations.* New York: McGraw-Hill. 2005.

Postal Addressing Standards 2. n.d.

Pratt, Mary K. ""6 Key Skills IT Grads Are Lacking." 25 February 2012. *http://www.networkworld.com/.* 2012 February 2012 <http://www.networkworld.com/news/2012/021312-6-key-skills-new-it-256051.html>.

"Readabilitiy." n.d. *en.wikipedia.org.* 5 February 2012 <http://en.wikipedia.org/wiki/Readability>.

Remillard, Brad. "How Recruiters Read Resumes In 10 Seconds or Less." 18 January 2010. *http://www.impacthiringsolutions.com/.* 2012 April 2012 <http://www.impacthiringsolutions.com/careerblog/2010/01/18/how-recruiters-read-resumes-in-10-seconds-or-less/>.

"RFP_CFXProfessionalServices.pdf." n.d. *www.virginiadot.org.* 2012 4 March <http://www.virginiadot.org/business/resources/const/RFP_CFXProfessionalServices.pdf>.

Russell, C. P. "How To Write A Sales-Making Letter." *Printer's Ink.* 2 June 1921.

Schramm, W. *How Communication Works.* Urbana: University of Illinois Press, 1954.

Shannon, C. E. & Weaver, W. *The Mathematical Theory of Communication.* Urbana: University of Illinois Press, 1949.

Sherman, L. A. *Analytics of Literature, a Manual for the Objective Study of English Prose and Poetry.* Boston: Ginn. 1893.

"The Visual Display of Quantitative Information." n.d. *http://www.edwardtufte.com.* 8 June 2012 <http://www.edwardtufte.com/tufte/books_vdqi>.

Thompson, Clive. "PowerPoint Makes You Dumb." 14 December 2003. *www.nytimes.com.* 31 March 2012 <http://www.nytimes.com/2003/12/14/magazine/2003-the-3rd-annual-year-in-ideas-powerpoint-makes-you-dumb.html>.

Thomson, Clive. "PowerPoint Makes You Dumb." 14 December 2003. *www.nytimes.com.* 31 March 2012 <http://www.nytimes.com/2003/12/14/magazine/2003-the-3rd-annual-year-in-ideas-powerpoint-makes-you-dumb.html>.

Tufte, E. R. (1997). *Visual and Statistical Thinking: Displays of Evidence for Making Decisions.* CT: Graphics Press USA.

Tufte, E. R. (2006). *The Cognitive Style of PowerPoint, 2nd edition.* CT: Graphics Press.

Wegner, M. and D. Girasek. 2003. "How readable are child safety seat installation instructions?" Pediatrics111:588-591.

Credits

Page 130. © 2010 L-Soft International, Inc. http://www.lsoft.com/resources/
pdf/wp-EmailMarketingBestPractices.pdf. August 25, 2010.

Index

A
acceptable use policy, (AUP), 26–27
active vs. passive voice, 69–71
adaptation, 64–65
adjustment grants, 95–97
AIDA approach, 100–101
assessments, 232

B
Bcc, 30–31
block style letter, 40
    sample text, 43
    template, 41–42
blogs, 32–33, 36, 53–54
bulk SMS, 32

C
career development, 244
Cc, 30–31
certifications, 212–213, 232–234
circular organizational chart, 12
clichès and idioms, 69
collaborative reports, 171–172
communicating in meetings, 187–190
communication
    cycle, 4, 5–10
    form and expectation, 25
    in the workplace, 198–199
confusing word pairs, 79
cover letters, 223–227

D
dangling modifers, 78
digital information literacy, 231–232
direct observation, 169
discriminatory language, 65–67

E
electronic portfolios, 220–222
e-mail, 28, 30–31, 34, 44, 49
    attachments, 31, 50
    marketing, 110–134
    template, 45
emphasis, 77–78
engaged employees, 4, 34
experimentation, 169
external mail, 29

F
feedback, and follow-up, 7, 9, 87–88
formal reports, 160–172

G
gender and age neutral language, 67–69
good will, 28, 34, 91, 95
good will messages, 97–99
group writing, 172–175

I
IM, 32, 52
internal mail, 29

internet, 27–28
interpersonal communication, 183–184
interview follow-up, 244
interviewing, 235, 237–243
intranet, 28

J
job search strategies, 234

M
misplaced modifiers, 78
modified block style letter, 44, 46–48

N
negative response to a routine inquiry, 94–95
networking, 235

O
online advertising, 110
oral presentations, 190–195
organizational culture, 10–11
o-rings, 183

P
paragraph length, 86
paragraph transitions, 83
parallelism and balance, 83–85
persuasive messages, 99–100
persuasive requests, 101–105
phone skills, 185–187
planning stages of writing, 37–38
positive response to a routine inquiry, 92–94
PowerPoint, 195–198
problem-solving process, the, 165–166

R
readability, 81
referencing methods, 164–165
reflective listening, 9, 10, 21
report
    cycle, 141–143
    format, 143–159

research methods, 166–167
resumes, 205–220
RFP proposals, 111, 136–137
routine inquiry, 91–92

S
salary and benefits, 243–244
sales
    campaigns, 108
    message, 105–107, 109
secondary data, 170–171
sentence
    clarity, 79–80
    design, 73–74
    fluency, 82
    length, 80–82
    organization, 75–77
short reports, 159–160
shuttle *Challenger,* 146, 183
slang, 65
SMS, 31, 51
social
    media, 110
    networking, 28, 35
soft skills, 3, 207, 209
standard organizational chart, 12
supporting examples, 77
surveys, 167–169

T
templates, 39, 150
text messages, 35, 49
transformational communication cycle, 18
twitter, 32, 52–53, 106, 232

U
URL, 28, 74, 134

W
word choice, 65